MODERN HUMANITIES RESEARCH ASSOCIATION
PUBLICATIONS OF THE MHRA
VOLUME 20

BREAKING WITH TRADITION
BELARUSIAN SHORT PROSE IN THE EARLY TWENTY-FIRST CENTURY

MODERN HUMANITIES RESEARCH ASSOCIATION

PUBLICATIONS OF THE
MODERN HUMANITIES RESEARCH ASSOCIATION

The prestigious Publications of the MHRA series is devoted to works of outstanding scholarly merit.

www.mhra.org.uk/series/pmhra

Breaking with Tradition

Belarusian Short Prose in the Early Twenty-First Century

Arnold McMillin

Modern Humanities Research Association
Publications of the MHRA 20
2018

Published by

The Modern Humanities Research Association
Salisbury House
Station Road
Cambridge CB1 2LA
United Kingdom

First published 2018

ISBN 978-1-78188-770-7

CONTENTS

INTRODUCTION

This survey of young Belarusian prose is in many ways a sequel to my 'last' book, which has come like an unexpected child or, in English tradition, Tosti's farewell.[1] Even shorter than its predecessor, *Spring Shoots*, it follows the same rough pattern of thematically arranged chapters, but makes less attempt to treat writers in only one chapter, preferring to allow some writers' works to appear in several different parts of the book. The scope is only short prose (*apaviadańni, apovieści*), although it has been frustrating not to be able to tackle novels, but — leaving art aside — *vita brevis*, or, as I once wrote, 'Small is Sometimes Beautiful.'[2] Once again debut writers rub shoulders with those of greater experience, and, as an observer from outside, I have tried, where possible, to praise rather than censure.

The aim of the book is to show some of the variety and imagination that young prose writers bring to their work, and to illustrate a pragmatic selection of some of the topics in which they are interested. As in my previous efforts, and even more so here, there is no pretence to anything like a full picture: with prose I have been particularly restricted by the books available in Britain, although, despite that, glad to have become acquainted with much lively and talented Belarusian writing in the course of my work. Naturally, some of the themes are far from country-specific (Love and sex; People and animals; Religion and philosophy) whilst others are highly relevant to contemporary Belarus (Leadership and the country; Writing; History), although all literature written in an oppressed and neglected language is in itself very important for the development of national culture and consciousness.

I hope that the more than usual references to my own earlier work will be seen as sentimental nostalgia rather than hubris. The epigraphs from Shakespeare, who was himself far from insular, are intended to bring a slightly broader context to my little book.

Sincerest thanks are due to Valiańcina Aksak, Jim Dingley, Voĺha Kalackaja, Gillian Long, Gerard Lowe and Źmicier Višnioŭ for their help, especially in locating texts of all kinds. As always, I am particularly indebted to Svetlana for her support, no matter what.

Arnold McMillin, November 2017

Notes to the Introduction

1. The reference is to a popular Victorian parlour song, Tosti's 'Goodbye' favoured by Australian singer Dame Nellie Melba who made a large number of 'farewell' appearances.
2. Arnold McMillin, 'Small is Sometimes Beautiful: Studying 'Minor' Languages at University with Particular Reference to Belarus: The Presidential Address of the Modern Humanities Research Association', *Modern Language Review*, 101.4 (2006), xxxii –xliii.

CHAPTER 1

Love, Sex and Loneliness

Shakespeare, 'loyal cantons of contemned love'
Twelfth Night, I, v, 264[1]

Love, sex and loneliness are ubiquitous in world literature, not least in young Belarusian poetry where in the present author's last book, *Spring Shoots*,[2] although the young poets were divided into rough thematic categories, love was so widespread a theme that it could not be given a category of its own. Eros and, more rarely, agape, as reflected in the short prose of the contemporary writers considered here, ranges from violence to sentimentality, emotional despair and confusion to fluid self-identity. Men and women alike write about their feelings, sometimes narrating from the point of view of the opposite sex, usually, but not always, about problematic relations with real or would-be lovers.

The theme of conflicting desires for sex and personal freedom is widespread, as, for instance, in 'Abarani maje sny' (Protect my dreams) by Stanislava Umiec (b. 1991), in which a detailed description of the young female narrator's life turns to troubled emotional entanglements, hardly clarified by her reading Janka Kupala's poem 'Jana i ja' (She and I, 1913); she sensibly reflects that it is crazy to fall for somebody you do not know, but nonetheless, dreams of declaring her love for a former close friend:

> І цяпер, выпусціўшы яго, я адчувала сябе вольнай і шчаслівай. Можа быць я нават паляцела б, але гарачыя рукі, абхапіўшыя мае плечы, вымусілі мяне застацца.[3]

> (And now, having let him go, I felt myself free and happy. Perhaps I would even have flown, but warm arms embracing my shoulders made me stay.)

Comparable to the title of Kupala's poem is that of a story by Jaŭhien Martynovič (b. 1985), 'jon i jana' (he and she) in which the female narrator describes how being together with her man has saved her from loneliness, but she is not at all certain they should remain together.[4]

Before turning to a writer who describes extensively some of the problems and miseries of love, it is worth quoting a quatrain written in 2013 by Taćciana Barysiuk (b. 1971) that might be considered terminally desperate or acceptance of miserable reality, apart, of course, from the subtitle:

Формула жаночага шчасця ў шлюбе
(*антыпарады*)
Муж здрадзіў? Б'е? Астыў? Няхай!
Трывай. Цярпі. Даруй. Кахай.
Забудзь пра талент, летуценні –
I стань яго маўклівым ценем.[5]

(A formula for female happiness (*some anti-advice*)
Your husband has betrayed you? He beats you? Has cooled? Let him.
Put up with it. Endure. Forgive. Love him.
Forget about talent, dreams –
And become his silent shadow.)

Maryja Roŭda (real name Salaŭjova, b. 1975), presents graphically in several stories from her *Kliničny vypadadak, albo Daremnyja ŭcioki* (A clinical case, or Fruitless flight),[6] the theme of women's loneliness and sexual obsession, often in conflict with her reluctance to give up freedom. Indeed, this often tense and harrowing book, swinging from one extreme to another, is among the most credible fictional accounts of the psychology of female sexuality that the present writer has ever read. The title story is one of the most bizarre, albeit rich in detail, in which the troubled narrator describes marriage to a German 'gnome' who, despite conflicting feelings of pity and dependence, cannot provide lasting happiness, particularly after the narrator has read his strange diaries, even if he might be a double of one of her earlier lovers (Roŭda, 161–64). This story demonstrates the author's imagination and skill when she describes her amorous feelings vividly as an abandoned book:

> А мне здавалася, што ўсё гэта — выпадкова прачытаная кніга, знойдзеная ў цягніку і няўмысна пакінутая для іншага пасажыра (Roŭda, 161).
>
> (And it seemed to me that all this was like a casually read book found in a train and deliberately left for another passenger.)

In another striking image the heroine, finding an abandoned orange, compares it to her own fate:

> Засохлы й закінуты, непатрэбны цяпер ужо нікому. Вось так і каханне хоць-калі, як апельсін, які своечасова не з'елі. Спачатку адкладалі на потым альбо пакідалі іншым. (Roŭda, 177)
>
> (Dried up and abandoned, now no longer needed by anybody. That is love at any time, like an orange that has not been eaten up promptly. First it was set aside for later or left for others.)

Describing her relations with men, she feels herself part of a dangerous game:

> Я як быццам бы гуляю ў найскладнейшую гульню й баюся прайграць. Але хто сказаў, што мужчына — мая самая галоўная партыя на шахматным полі жыцця? (Roŭda, 181)

(It is as if I am playing a most complex game and am afraid of losing. But who said that a man was my main opponent on the chess board of life?)

'Niama Soni paratunku' (No salvation for Sonia), from which the last quotation is taken, is an emblematic story of strong feelings and weak will-power. Of her lover Kiryl, the narrator says:

> І дагэтуль я ніяк не магла атрымаць ад яго асалоду, таму што я толькі тое й рабіла, што балансавала між каханнем і свабодай і не ведала, што выбраць, не ведала, ці трэба выбіраць. (Roŭda, 185)

> (And up to then I could not get any sweet pleasure from him, because all I did was balance between love and freedom, and did not know which to choose, I did not know whether I had to make a choice.)

The story ends with a resolution simply to begin life... (Roŭda, 187)

The third element, in addition to sexual passion and freedom is, not unexpectedly, loneliness, the worst feeling of all (Roŭda, 185). At the beginning of 'Znajomy nieznajomiec' (A familiar stranger) from his *Dziciačy manifiest (Apovieść i apaviadańni)* (A children's manifesto [A novella and stories]), Kiryl Stasieĺka (b. 1990) through his narrator ponders the reality and unreality of love, the latter being perhaps mainly an escape from loneliness, as he remarks, observing the older generation:

> ... яны ўсе пабраліся не таму, што мелі асаблівыя пачуцці адно да аднаго, а каб не застацца на ўсё жыццё адзінокімі.[7]

> (...they all got together not because they had special feelings for each other but in order not to remain lonely for all their lives.)

In another story, 'Natatki ekspierymientatara' (Notes of an experimenter) the eponymous narrator associates loneliness with strength:

> Толькі моцная асоба можа свядома вытрымаць пакуты адзіноты. Каханне і сяброўства выдуманыя, каб было прасцей жыць, каб чалавек не адчуваў сябе адзінокім. (Stasieĺka, 178)

> (Only a strong person can consciously bear the torments of loneliness. Love and friendship have been thought up to make it easier to live, so that a person should not feel themselves lonely.)

The female narrator of 'Apteka' (The Pharmacy) by Arciom Kavalieŭski (b. 1979) decides that there is no medicine for loneliness, and, after hopefully seeking the company of chemists, concludes that her loneliness has closed her off from the whole world.[8]

Vaĺžyna Mort (b. 1981) has a very individual approach to the theme of loneliness: in 'Adzinota — mužčynskaha rodu... (Loneliness is of male gender), for instance, she memorably expresses her resentment at living in a phallocentric world:

> Адзінота — мужчынскага роду. Нягледзячы на тое, што пра яе кажуць 'яна', я ўпэўненая, што бачыла яе велізарны пэніс. Фалас адзіноты, падобны да падзорнай трубы. Як толькі яна заўважае, як я недалёк, ціхая й непрывабная зь дзьвюмя заколкамі ў танклявых валасах яна раскладае гэтую трубу да патрэбных размераў і глядзіць у яе, назірае за мною праз павелічальнае шкло свайго пэніса.[9]
>
> (Loneliness is of male gender. Despite the fact that they call it 'she', I am sure that I have seen its immense penis. The phallus of loneliness is like a telescope. As soon as it notices that I have appeared somewhere near, quiet and unattractive with two clips in my fine hair, it opens this tube to the necessary size and looks in it, watching me through the magnifying glass of its penis.)

At the end of Mort's piece, this ubiquitous loneliness even creeps up quietly as she is attending her mother's death bed, leading her to neglect the washing-up, as she cannot do it just for herself (Mort, 68).

Before leaving Mort in this chapter, it is worth mentioning that venereal disease does not seem to be a factor in the various accounts of tormented love, and when she boldly begins one unnamed piece, 'U mianie tripper...' (I have got the clap) the subject is treated lightly, beginning with reflections on the (Belarusian version of) the word's origin, and ending with her apparently not very bright lover Ivan, who imagines that the word means a certain breed of dog (Mort, 84–87).

One short but very unusual contribution to the theme of love and loneliness is by someone who only refers to herself by the pseudonym Marta, 'List pra kachańnie' (A letter about love), in which she advises women to marry not for love, but rationally, without illusions, although the alternative of loneliness is clearly implied.[10] Earlier in this heartfelt epistle she writes about praying for a conscious Belarusian (she did not want anyone who was mentally a Russian), but when she meets a young man who fulfils her national credentials and teaches him to speak Belarusian, after they have had children she soon feels she is living in a grave and cannot even look at him (Marta, 154–55).

No more successful in finding happiness is the narrator of 'Mara pra pryhožaje kachańnie' (A dream of beautiful love) by Andruś Danilievič (b. 1990). The (male) narrator is toyed with by a woman who seems more interested in competing with other women than in responding to a shy young man, in any case preferring experience to timidity in the opposite sex.[11] In another story by the same author 'Upieršyniu...' (For the first time...), a young boy is obsessed by a glamorous teacher, but, naturally can only make gauche efforts to attract her attention (Danilievič, 77–78). Male timidity is also featured in some stories by Jaŭhien Martynovič, such as 'Viartańnie' (The return) and 'Ja prosta chaču ciabie ŭbačyć' (I simply want to see you), as well as in 'Śviatlo i ciemra' (Light and dark) by another young writer Hanna Šybut (b. 1993), which shows a relationship plagued by youthful shyness, portraying events (or lack of them) through the eyes of first Viera and then Miša, in stories of those names, which are somewhat marred by the author's inclination to sentimentality.[12] There is, however, nothing sentimental in a piece entitled 'racyjanalizm' (rationalism) from *Šali* (Scales) a book of lyrical-everyday prose by Źmicier Bajarovič (d.o.b. unknown)[13] in which the narrator describes his desire to live with a fat, highly domesticated woman who will wait on him hand and foot, while he sings and writes poetry on the balcony, and she performs domestic tasks, such as carrying the rubbish out. The closing words sum up this blatantly selfish philosophy:

> І мы будзем жыць разам шчасліва: адзін без аднаго.
> А любіць я буду цябе.[14]

> (And we shall live happily together: one without the other. / But I will love you.)

Other of Bajarovič's miniatures describe less crude, albeit sometimes strange, treatment of women. 'Kachańnie' (Love), for instance, offers a detailed picture of the coming of dawn, concluding that switching off the light reflects an important change in a relationship: 'Так закаханасць змяняецца каханнем' (Thus, being in love turns to love) (Bajarovič, 23). Odder is 'vajna' (war) which describes two warring librarians who suspend hostilities only when the narrator returns an overdue book, leading one of them to threaten expulsion. It produces an unexpected response from the customer: 'А я ўжо гатовы быў узняць белы сцяг. І аддаць ёй душу' (Bajarovič, 27) (And I was quite ready to raise a white flag. And surrender my soul to her). Even more bizarre is 'prapanova' (the proposal), in which, instead of offering the usual entertainments to his girlfriend, he invites her to his room:

> І ў пакоі:
>
> Я скажу, каб ты села на зэдлік.
> І ты будзеш сядзець на зэдліку.
> А потым мы ажэнімся. (Bajarovič, 34)

> (And in the room: // I shall tell you to sit on a stool. / And you will sit on the stool. / And then we shall get married.)

The same author's 'navuka' (a lesson), however, slightly modifies the impression that all his poems about interpersonal relations are bizarre: 'Аднойчы ты навучыла мяне кахаць. Таму я больш не кахаю нікога' (Bajarovič, 54) (Once you taught me how to love. For that reason I do not love anybody else). Finally may be mentioned a miniature, 'Liubaja, liubaja' (Dearest, dearest) in which dreams of repeating their parents' happiness leads, after several children, to nothing but washing powder (Bajarovič, 72).

Before turning to descriptions of extreme male selfishness, it may be worth mentioning a few other texts. Several stories in *Padarunak dlia Adeli* (A present for Adelia) by Sieviaryn Kviatkoŭski (b. 1973) concern sex in one way or another; in 'Majskaja saha' (May saga) a Polish teacher tells his students about his experiences during World War II (this story is discussed in Chapter 6).[15] Another piece, 'Śvietka' is named after a woman of easy virtue whose main pleasure seems to be having her back (and not only that) washed by a man (Kviatkoŭski, 70–74). Siarhiej Balachonaŭ (b. 1977) is best known for his imaginative and entertaining major work, combining elements of historical and detective novels, *Imia hrušy* (The name of the pear), but who has also produced a handful of stories, one of which relates to the present theme, 'Paliavańnie na pačvarnaha parsiuka: Zlaja miaščanskaja pryhoda XVI vieku' (Hunting a freakish boar: An evil bourgeois adventure from the 16th century). It concerns a love triangle that is rudely interrupted, not by an aggrieved consort but by a monstrously ugly boar which pursues the central character, Liudavika, relentlessly. This is somewhat beyond her extensive previous experience, as we read in the following excerpt:

> Гукалі, дзей яна яшчэ ня быўшы ўдавіцаю, чыніла любы з Данілам, але ж ня толькі зь ім, а яшчэ з цэлым рэестрам віленскіх мяшчанаў, жаўнераў ды нават, даруй Божа, сьвятароў трох канфэсій хрысьціянскіх.[16]
>
> (People used to say that even before she had become a widow, she made love with Danila, and not only with him but with a whole range of Vilnia burghers, soldiers and, even, God forgive us, with priests of all three Christian confessions as well.)

These diverse stories reflect a world that, though real, is very different from contemporary problems and neuroses.

Two other stories may also be mentioned here: a humorous *jeu d'esprit* by Paval Kaściukievič (b. 1979), 'Ja kachaju ciabie, Julija' (I love you, Julia),[17] which begins with a discussion of the names of Caesar's children, leading to a serious quarrel (like Shakespeare's Montagues and Capulets) about names, and suggesting the play's real title should be *Romeo and Julia*. Unlike the bard's play, however, it ends with a relatively happy ending of mutual love, albeit tempered by a mysterious reluctance to end the account of this relationship. Also of some interest is the story 'Ščaślivaja' (The happy woman) by Arciom Kavalieŭski in which the female narrator, obsessed by a man, comes to realize that: '... час абумоўлены дзвюма толькі рэчамі: жаданнем прыналежнасці й немагчымасцю яе здзейсніць' (Kavalieŭski, 125–26)[18] (time is conditioned by only two things: the desire to belong and the impossibility of achieving that). At the end, however, quite unlike many of the unhappy and troubled women discussed earlier, she declares categorically that now she is happy. Quite different is Kavalieŭski's story 'Malako' (Milk), where the liquid of the title is the background for a phantasmagorical tale of drinking (in beer cellars) as a man's prelude to love making (Kavalieŭski, 105).

The exclusively male point of view in *Pomnik atručanym liudziam* (A monument to poisoned people) by Siarhiej Kalienda (b. 1985) presents more than once the idea that women are essentially men's possessions, although in 'Z taboju ja nikoli nie pamru' (With you I shall never die) the narrator states that keeping a woman in this way is no way to achieve true love:

> Ён усё жыццё жадаў толькі яе, ён імкнуўся да валодання ёю, сляпога валодання, але ж гэта забівае каханне.[19]

> (All his life he only desired her, he strove to possess her, to gain blind possession, but this is just what kills love.)

Most memorably, however, Kalienda writes freely through one of his characters, a journalist named Frank, about keeping a girl captive and regarding himself as her unseen *haspadar* (lord) and *uladar* (owner). Such a situation is, unfortunately, far from rare in backward and/or patriarchal societies, as is the division of women by men, noted by Voĺha Hapiejeva in her introduction to Kalienda's debut book, into sexually loose sluts and prostitutes contrasted with idealized female figures beyond the realistic reach of men (Kalienda, 5). In fact, most of the women in Kalienda's writing are, to use an ugly word, objectified. A strange and for most people disgusting form of intimacy is described in 'Vanity' (Vomiting). For more detail see Chapter 4, which contains a section devoted to squalor.

A word should be said about various kinds of fantasy as it relates to love. In its simplest, rather comic, form in 'Trubačka' (The little tube) by Kiryl Duboŭski (b. 1983), the narrator encounters a girl with a tube protruding from her head into which he pours beer, but their closeness does not last; nor does it work with other girls with tubes, so he gets his own little tube and finds himself full of the affection and love that he had not received from the opposite sex.[20] More subtle fantasies are two stories that show how men seeking closeness with glamorous women or, indeed, men are, in fact, looking for themselves. In one story from Alisa Biziajeva's 'Zdani prytomnaści' (Ghosts of consciousness), 'Dziaŭčynka na prypynku' (Girl at a tram stop), for instance, the male narrator follows the girl and eventually persuades her to visit his flat. Saying little, she performs many domestic jobs, including making coffee and delicious dinners, during which they watch films on the television. When she sleeps alone on the couch he can only admire her, but when she eventually disappears, he learns that this ideal woman was, in fact, none other than himself.[21] A comparable transformation occurs in two stories by Kiryl Stasieĺka, 'Son? Reaĺnaść?' (A Dream? Reality?) and the already mentioned 'Znajomy nieznajomiec'. In the first of them the narrator, falling asleep in the theatre, seems, amongst other things, to escape from a wedding to a woman he does not love, and to go through one of the multiple doors in the story, meeting himself, but twenty years older. It had just been a vivid dream (Stasieĺka, 99–109). In the second story the narrator becomes fascinated by a socially successful but rather feckless student whom he observes obsessively until he sees him being betrayed by his glamorous girlfriend. Before long, however, he discovers that he has been observing himself (Stasieĺka, 110–26). In the same author's 'Zvyčajnaja liuboŭ' (Everyday love) amorous feelings appear to make the narrator gradually become more humane to others, but when at the end his beloved reappears, she declares that his love was not real:

> Маё імя Эгаістыка, я ёсць горшая частка твайго 'Я', я — гэта ты сам. Заўсёды ты любіў толькі сябе, але не разумеў гэтага (Stasieĺka, 159).
>
> (My name is Egoist, I am the worst part of your 'I', I am you yourself. You always loved only yourself, but did not understand that)

Džeci (Viera Burlak, b. 1977) in an interesting story 'Jaźminičny Kaliadki' (Jasmine's Christmas),[22] combines fantasy (e.g. a hammer that makes people fall in and out of love at single strokes) with characteristic humour and realism that changes to fantasy and back again rapidly. A strange house and mysterious love-making are part of this fantasy, although the ending, in which the narrator does not know who the father of her daughter Runia is, has a distinctly modern feel (Džeci, 124).

Also worth mentioning is a bizarre story of changing identity by Larysa Palazkova (b. 1977), 'Liustravy čalaviek' (Man in a mirror), in which, on waking up, the eponymous character sees in a mirror a middle-aged man who soon changes into an old woman. After various other transformations, he leaps away from the mirror, now finding he is a young woman.[23] Also relevant here is a piece by Anka Upala (pen-name of Aliena Kazlova, b. 1981), 'Iń — Jan (pieraapranańnie ŭ hiendernyja stereatypy)' (Ying and Yang [A re-dressing as gender stereotypes]) which describes a group of talented girls, one of whom, ignored by the others, thinks of herself as a man.[24]

* * * * *

There is nothing fantastic about gay love, nor is it transgressive, like the behaviour described in many of Kalienda's works, for example, although many backward people regard homosexual relations as, at the very least, unnatural. The Belarusian leader, for instance, informed the German foreign minister, Guido Westerweller on an official visit to Miensk in 2012, that it was better to be a dictator than gay. Such is the background to the last two texts to be discussed here. The explicitly lesbian poetry of Nasta Mancevič (b. 1983) was considered in *SS*.[25] Unsurprisingly, the prose in her first book shares the same concerns and longings as the verse, but, perhaps expectedly, aroused more indignation and accusations of pornography than the poems. In England of yesteryear, for instance, it was usually not poetry but books of prose that appeared before courts, accused of obscenity.[26] Mancevič's world is one of squalor and lust, described with a mixture of humour and disgust, but the great difference between her stories and several of the male writers in this chapter is that there is no inherent or assumed inequality between the sexual partners. Incidentally, some of the stories appear to have masculine narrators, although this does not seem to affect the semantics. Mancevič writes in a clear laconic style that may have added to the aggression she aroused when the book first came out. Only about half the stories are devoted to sexual encounters, and these are mainly quite explicit. Some are more mysterious, like, for instance 'Pazl' (Puzzle) about a girl spitting tea onto the window of a crowded trolleybus, which the narrator condones on discovering that the man in front has only one eye: 'I я адчула, што ўсё харашо' (Mancevič, 18) (And I felt that everything was alright). 'Paranoja' (Paranoia) describes a man's terrifying journey home in the dark, during which he is set upon by hooligans; when he reaches the entrance to his building he sees a girl go in, and in a fit of paranoia puts his hand over her mouth, saying 'Паспрабуй толькі піскнуць, шлюха' (Mancevič, 28) (Just try and utter a squeak, you slag). The author often looks back to her childhood: 'Doždž' (Rain) comprises reminiscences of this time and her early perception of sounds (Mancevič, 3–4), and the title story 'Ptuški' (Birds) describes many childish dreams and fantasies. Eventually she comes back to Viliejka and has to ask for work from a woman who loves her and whom she loves. After sex, the story ends thus:

> Мы ляжым, цяжка дыхаем і ўсміхаемся. 'Дык вось ты, аказваецца, якая', — кажа яна (Mancevič, 13)
>
> (We lie, breathing heavily and smiling. 'So that's what you are like', she says)

Finally, an untitled story reflects on the idea that only death gives life meaning, offering several counter-arguments, for example, the last drops of beer in a bottle in front of the television, compared with when, as a six-year-old girl, she saw from her bedroom window their alcoholic neighbour being buried and felt happy (Mancevič, 31). Nasta Mancevič's open descriptions of casual sex are less shocking than male dreams of domination or, indeed, the violence and squalor of the life beyond her personal experiences that are described with a laconism that remains in the memory longer than more extravagant outpourings. Similarly, her use of mild swear words such as *srany* (shitty) to describe aspects of her environment are no less effective than the use of 'strong' words by some male writers, with or without ellipses.

Uladź Harbacki (b. 1978), a native of Viciebsk who works at the European Humanities University in Vilnia, is a talented scholar[27] as well as an interesting writer of prose describing his own realization of various aspects of life, including sexuality in *Pieśni traliejbusnych rahuliaŭ: Kazki i proza žyćcia* (Songs of the trolleybus poles. Fairytales and the prose of life, 2016).[28] The book is a semi-fictitious account of his early life and feelings. Written in lively contemporary Belarusian with a strong admixture of Viciebsk dialect, it is more than a very honest confession, but also an attempt to imagine the feelings of those around him (like, for instance, L.N. Tolstoi in his *Detstvo* [Childhood, 1852]).[29] The three mainstays of Harbacki's early life described here are the discoveries of the Belarusian language, of his gayness, and of his atheism, all of which set him apart from the surrounding culture in Viciebsk. The variegated forms of writing in this book include *kazki* ([fairy] tales) related by his granny, a letter, realism with elements of fantasy, and frank confession of his beliefs, discoveries and desires. Loneliness has been a major theme in this chapter. In Harbacki's case, however, it is not simply the result of despair or narrow introspection — his narrative also takes on the wider world, for instance, recent events on the Maidan.

If the first *kazka* was about discovering the Belarusian language, the second is about the realization that he is gay, and he gives a detailed and honest description of how he discovered this, coming to believe firmly that the fate of gays lies in their own hands. A number of excerpts will provide examples of Harbacki's experience of love. 'Pieršy raz' (Harbacki, 35–36) (The first time) is a fairly detailed account of the first experience of gay sex in which he discovers new uses for various parts of his body, as the following passage makes clear in a spirit of wonder at a new world:

> А як забыць пра эксплёзію эмоцыяў, спазмы раптам пасталелага, цалкам дарослага цела? Як доўга яшчэ трэба было прызвычайвацца да новага, схаванага, хоць і ўсім дарослым вядомага досьведу... Вусны, аказваецца, павінны ня толькі піць воду, але і цалаваць, піць іншага, рукі патрэбныя былі ня толькі вітацца, але і мацаць, вандраваць па целе, у целе іншага, нос патрэбны, аказваецца, ня толькі ўдыхаць, але казытаць шыю, грудзі, азадак іншага, а язык быў не толькі, каб паказваць яго злой і зьвяглівай суседцы, але каб лашчыць смачнае і бясконцу паміралае, на вачох адцьвіталае чалавечае цела... (Harbacki, 35–36)

> (And how can I forget the explosion of emotions, the spasms of a suddenly mature fully adult body? How much longer was it to take to become familiar with a new, hidden, although known to all grown-ups, experience... The mouth, it turns out, was not only for drinking water, but for kissing, for drinking from another person, hands were not only for greeting, but for exploring, wandering over a body and inside another's body, one's nose, it turns out, is not only for breathing in, but for tickling the neck, breast, bum of another person, and my tongue not only for sticking out at an evil and annoying neighbour, but in order to lick the delicious and endlessly dying human body, fading before your eyes...)

His fate was foreseen several times by his grandmother: in 'Hadańnie pa kartam' (Reading the cards) where she predicted a difficult love life ahead for her grandson (Harbacki, 43–47); in 'Cyhanka' (The gypsy woman) a Romany fortune teller on a train, to the consternation of other passengers, warns him of betrayal and accuses him of letting down many girls cruelly, before he declares his gayness and tells her to become more up-to-date (Harbacki, 49–54). In some respects his stories recall the bleaker side of Mancevič's prose. In 'Źbićcio' (Beating up), for instance, he presents a bleak picture of Viciebsk where there is nothing for young people to do (Harbacki, 66), although his feelings towards this ancient city are very mixed.[30] He constantly thinks of his distant lover in another, easier, country, and when a child draws attention to his scent on a trolleybus, it leads to hostility and aggression from the other passengers. Later, a beating up by three hooligans outside his flat leads him to reflect on other victims of society's morality: girls, he knows, may be beaten up by men for various reasons, but gays are mostly attacked precisely because of their sexual orientation (Harbacki, 74–75). An unusual story is 'Tramvajnica' (The tram driver) which gives a vivid picture of life in this part of the transport system. When the drivers praise their children, Nadzieja, the driver of the title, mentions her boy who is living with a man; the drivers are more surprised by her frankness than shocked, but later become colder towards her. Seeing male couples at stops, she thinks of her son in another town and weeps. But she is still alive (Harbacki, 83–88). To end this brief review of Harbacki's book, the story 'Viasnovy čmut' (The spring cheat) gives a vivid picture of the effect of April (the eponymous cheat); the author begins his description with the emancipating smells after winter. One short quotation will suffice:

> Раз на год пахі зямныя і пахі чалавечыя ўзмацняюцца і дурманяць людзей у палоне хэнці. У сёлетнім красавіку зьвялі нас пахі і жаданьні, самоту так удала і прыгожа аздаблялыя, дапаўнялыя. Двух самотніх мальцаў, вясёлых і сьмелых геяў. Вясновы чмут штурхнуў нас з самоты вонкі, і мы знайшліся, як знаходзяцца хіба згаладалыя, сасмаглыя ля выратавальнага, нечакана знойдзенага калодзежа. (Harbacki, 37)
>
> (Once a year earthly and human scents grow stronger and intoxicate people possessed by desire. In this year's April, scents and longing brought us together, so successfully and beautifully enhancing and embellishing our loneliness. Two lonely young men, merry and bold gays. The spring cheat pushed us out of our loneliness, and we found ourselves like starving, thirsty people near a life-saving unexpectedly discovered well.)

Finally, it may be noted that although the sexual act itself has often been described in world literature as funny or grotesque, the theme of inter-sexual relations has not often been treated in a purely comic way in young Belarusian prose. An exception, however, is Džeci's story mentioned above.

* * * * *

Loneliness is not only related to love and sex, as it is in the work of Martynovič, Roŭda, Stasieĺka, Marta and Harbacki considered above. The theme will also occur occasionally in later chapters, but there are some writers, including Charužka, Kalienda and Stasieĺka, who describe vividly or have strong views on loneliness in general. For instance, Aliaksiej Charužka in a neurotic monologue 'Adzinota' (Loneliness) writes about insecurity, doubts, delusions and illusions, asking many questions of himself. The following short quotation about his imagining that someone is on the other side of his door before he discovers, looking for keys, that the keyhole has disappeared, will serve as a brief illustration of one young man's paranoia and, ultimately, loneliness:

> Хоць з чаго я ўзяў, што там ёсць чалавек? Што ува мне яго вызначыла? Прага цеплыні й пяшчоты ці страх адзіноты?[31]
>
> (Although where did I get the idea from that there was a person there? What sign of it was there within me? A longing for warmth and affection or fear of loneliness?)

In Siarhiej Kalienda's story 'Horad' (The city) the narrator, a heavy drinker, feels such loneliness that, in the search for company of any kind, he looks in at people's windows, not yet realizing that loneliness is universal (Kalienda, 38–39). The drunken 'hero' of his 'Samota' (Loneliness), Zakliopkin, enjoys playing dead and finds happiness in being treated by a non-judgmental doctor. It is only by being on the verge of death that he can gain the attention of his fellow-men. This, for him, is the essence, of life (Kalienda, 54–55). In a violent dream the narrator of 'Ci jość žyccio na miesiacy?' (Is there life on the moon?) sees a woman committing suicide in her bath because she is lonely (Kalienda, 70), which is a not untypical image from this writer's poisoned world.

Finally, in a story by Kiryl Stasieĺka 'Adzinota' (Loneliness) 60-year-old Vasiĺ has no family, friends or money. He draws a picture of a young man on his steamed-up window that disappears with the sun. Vasiĺ does not know what to do, lies down and dies (Stasieĺka, 189).

* * * * *

The wide variety of literature about the relations between or within the sexes in still patriarchal Belarus presents a picture of life where nothing is easy but where it is perhaps particularly difficult to have a satisfactory relationship where there is no equality between the partners, whoever they are and whatever their orientation. Loneliness, a frequent theme, is sometimes presented as being worse than the most unsatisfactory emotional bonds.

The young writers in this chapter have brought many talents to the universal themes of intimacy and inner torment, presenting an undoubtedly interesting, if at times depressing, body of worthwhile literature.

Notes to Chapter 1

1. This and all subsequent references to Shakespeare are from *The Arden Shakespeare: Complete Works*, ed. by Richard Proudfoot, Ann Thompson and David Scott Kastan (London, New Delhi, New York, Sydney: Bloomsbury, 1998).
2. Arnold McMillin, *Spring Shoots: Young Belarusian Poets in the Early Twenty-First Century*, Publications of the Modern Humanities Research Association, 19 (Cambridge: MHRA, 2015) (hereafter *SS*).
3. Stanislava Umiec, 'Abarani maje sny', in *Moj dzień pačynajecca: Proza i paezija maladych*, comp. by Viktar Šnip (Minsk: Mastackaja litaratura, 2015) (hereafter *Mdp*), pp. 283–91 (p. 291).
4. Jaŭhien Martynovič, 'jon i jana', *Mdp*, pp. 197–98.
5. Taćciana Barysiuk, 'Formula žanočaha ščaścia ŭ šliubie (*antyparada*)', *Litaraturny ekvatar: Aĺmanach*, 5 (2016), 25.
6. Maryja Roŭda, *Kliničny vypadak, aĺbo Daremnyja ŭcioki* (Minsk: Knihazbor, 2015) (hereafter Roŭda).
7. Kiryl Stasieĺka, *Dziciačy manifiest* (Minsk: Halijafy, 2015) (hereafter Stasieĺka), p. 110.
8. Arciom Kavalieŭski, *Addalienaść i addanaść* (Minsk: Halijafy, 2008) (hereafter Kavalieŭski), pp. 113–16.
9. Vaĺžyna Mort, *Ja tonieńkaja jak tvaje viejki* (Minsk: Lohvinaŭ, 2005) (hereafter Mort), p. 67.
10. Marta, 'List pra kachańnie', in *Žančyny vychodziać z-pad kantroliu: Bielaruskaje žanočaje apaviadańnie*, comp. by Natalka Babina and others (Minsk: Lohvinaŭ, 2007) (hereafter *Žvzpk*), pp. 153–57 (hereafter Marta), p.156.
11. Andruś Danilievič, 'Mara pra pryhožaje kachańnie', *Mdp*, pp.74–76 (hereafter Danilievič).
12. Hanna Šybut, 'Śviatlo i ciemra', *Mdp*, pp. 328–31 (hereafter Šybut).
13. Hereafter where the dates of birth of young prose writers are not given it is because they were not available at the time of writing.
14. Źmicier Bajarovič, *Šali* (Minsk: Halijafy, 2012) (hereafter Bajarovič), pp. 16–17.
15. Sieviaryn Kviatkoŭski, *Padarunak dlia Adeli* (Minsk: Lohvinaŭ, 2012) (hereafter Kviatkoŭski), pp. 33–43.
16. Siarhiej Balachonaŭ, *Imia hrušy* (Minsk: Lohvinaŭ, 2005) (hereafter Balachonaŭ), pp. 140–41.
17. Paval Kaściukievič, *Zbornaja RB pa niehaloŭnych vidach sportu* (Minsk: Lohvinaŭ, 2011) (hereafter Kaściukievič), pp. 22–27.
18. The title but not the tone of Kavalieŭski's story recalls a poem by Nadzieja Filon, '"Ščaślivaja", mnie kažuć liudzi ŭślied...' ('A happy one', so people say after me...) in which the poet declares herself unconditionally happy: *Kropli śviatla* (Minsk: TAA 'Charviest', 2012), p. 3.
19. Siarhiej Kalienda, *Pomnik atručanym liudziam* (Minsk: Halijafy, 2009) (hereafter Kalienda), p. 59.
20. Kiryl Duboŭski, 'Trubačka', in *Hienijuš loci: Konkurs maladych litaratараŭ da stahoddzia Larysy Hienijuš*, comp. by A. Chadanovič (Minsk: Lohvinaŭ, 2012) (hereafter *Hienijuš loci*), p. 86.
21. Alisa Biziajeva, 'Zdani prytomnaści'. *Dziejasloŭ*, 2(81) (2016), 180–83.
22. Džeci, 'Jaźminičny Kaliadki', *Žvzpk*, pp. 114–24 (hereafter Džeci).
23. Larysa Palazkova, 'Dva apaviadańni', *Maladość*, 1 (2005), 8–10 (pp. 9–10).
24. Anka Upala, *Dreva Entalipt* (Minsk: Lohvinaŭ, 2012) (hereafter Upala), pp. 68–71.
25. Nasta Mancevič, *Ptuški* (Minsk: Lohvinaŭ, 2012) (hereafter Mancevič).
26. Probably the most famous was D. H. Lawrence's *Lady Chatterley's Lover*, written and

first published outside Britain in the 1920s, which came before the courts when it appeared in England in 1960. Acquitted, it rapidly acquired some three million readers. Nasta Mancevič's book appeared in an edition of only three hundred copies, but at least she did not have to wait forty years before it was published in her own country.

27. See, for instance, his innovative *Hid pa feminizacyi bielaruskaj movy (Nomina agentis i niekatorych inšych asabovych naminacyjaŭ* (Vilnia: belarusians.co uk, 2016), an updated version of his earlier *Ab feminizacyi bielaruskaj movy: Feminizacyja nomina agentis i peŭnych inšych katehoryjaŭ u sučasnaj bielaruskaj movie* (Leicester: belarusians.co.uk, 2012).
28. Uladź Harbacki, *Pieśni traliejbusnych rahuliaŭ* (London: belarusians.co.uk, 2016) (hereafter Harbacki).
29. The author himself would doubtless laugh at such a remote comparison.
30. A semi-fantastic description of the city and what it might be is to be found in 'Baryśka' (Harbacki, 101–04).
31. Aliaksiej Charužka, 'Adzinota', *Pamiž*, 4 (2004–05), 54–58 (p. 54).

CHAPTER 2

The World and Its Inhabitants: Humans, Fish, Animals and Birds

1. The Seven Ages of Man

SHAKESPEARE, 'Like as the waves make towards the pebbled shore
So do our minutes hasten to their end'
Sonnets 60, 1–2

'man is the "paragon of animals"'
Hamlet, II, ii, 30

'the fishermen that walk upon the beach
Appear like mice'
King Lear, IV, vi, 17–18

This chapter hardly covers all the seven ages of man, leaving the fourth and fifth to other parts of the book. But here there are several different views of childhood, sometimes seen through memory, and a variety of descriptions of ageing and death. None of the latter, however, is nearly so grim as that at the end of Shakespeare's famous speech, 'All the world's a stage, / And all the men and women merely players...', which ends with some of the most gloomy lines in English literature describing old age and death:

Last scene of all,
That ends this strange eventful history,
Is second childishness, and mere oblivion,
Sans teeth, sans eyes, sans taste, sans everything.[1]

Elsewhere in this book there are elements of childhood where the child is a witness to cruel and incomprehensible things, such as 'Jak zakopvali duby' (How they dug up the oaks, 2011) by Aliaksiej Palačanski,[2] which is described in Chapter 4. There are, however, several other stories that bring childhood alive in various ways. As a parody of Marx, Kiryl Stasieĺka in 'Dziciačy manifiest (1849 hod, Londan) (A children's manifesto [London, 1849]) calls on children to rise up against the tyranny of grown-ups; the beginning of the story will give the flavour:

> Дарагія таварышы Дзеці! Дарослыя нам хлусяць, прыгнятаюць, прымушаюць. Так жыць больш нельга. Мы мусім выступіць адзіным фронтам і скінуць свае рабскія кайданы. (Stasielka, 148–50)
>
> (Dear comrade Children! Adults lie, oppress and coerce. We cannot continue like that. We must come forward in a united front and cast off the shackles of our slavery.)

Two very different stories about childhood share the same title 'Źnička' (Shooting star): Andruś Danilievič describes a boy making reluctant progress towards school wondering at the beauty and power of nature. When asked by a scornful teacher about stars, he only answers that they are beautiful and that anyone who catches a shooting star will be lucky. Although he is mocked, the boy knows that his words are true (Danilievič, 76–77). The story by Aleś Byčkoŭski (b. 1975) with the same title is, like so much of his prose, essentially science fiction.[3] In it a ten-year-old boy finds a black toy car, which he imagines to be connected with a shooting star he had seen recently and names Źnička. He dreams of taking it out to play where it performs all sorts of tricks (such as showing pictures of other people and lands) (Byčkoŭski, 87). Having accidentally pressed a black knob, he receives a message that the world will end in five minutes. After an alarming countdown the car's screen goes blank and the whole world is deserted, but suddenly the boy hears Źnička inviting him to go on a journey (Byčkoŭski, 88).

The remaining accounts or reminiscences of childhood mostly centre on the age of 12–13, that is the cusp of puberty. Anatoĺ Ivaščanka (b. 1981) in the first section, 'Pach voli' (The smell of liberty), of his *Anatalohija*,[4] describes the life of children of this age growing up in the Yeltsin years when the post-Soviet economy was in tatters. Whilst most were interested mainly in cigarettes and porn, a poor friend, Saša, stands apart, and later gets a job rather than staying on at school. In this quasi-factual narration, Ivaščanka recalls this youth mainly by the smell of unwashed linen which at the time he associated with liberty (Ivaščanka, 10). Jaŭhien Martynovič in 'Siem rečaŭ, jakija ja nie budu rabić, kali vyrastu!: List u budučyniu' (Seven things I shall not do when I grow up!: A letter to the future)[5] the narrator at the age of thirteen notes seven points in his parents' behaviour that he will not imitate: buying a razor; swilling the last mouthful of tea around his mouth; ringing around his child's more talented friends in order to get the answers for his homework; shopping for summer clothes in winter; cutting hair with scissors; providing a commentary on sport or the news on television; leaving a child alone in a queue. Such a catalogue of negatives provides its own picture of the life of at least one young teenager.

The recollections of children and childhood by Kryścina Banduryna (b. 1992) are somewhat grimmer. 'Śliady na čystaj papiery' (Traces on a blank sheet of paper)[6] begins with an account of how the narrator finds herself the focus of attention of a naughty young girl from whom she finds it difficult to free herself, despite valuing the girl's strong affection (Banduryna, 29–30). This leads to memories of how she, at the age of nine, was smuggled by her granny into a group of Chernobyl children who had been invited to stay with an apparently wealthy family in Ireland. Wrongly accused of trying to steal money, and with no language to explain herself she is branded a criminal, and not invited back the following year. The conclusion, as she recalls the other little girls and the original girl's look of trust and affection, is that it is difficult to remember what you particularly want (Banduryna, 32). This story is a vivid example of victimhood, but also of the gulf in understanding between many adults and children.

The middle ages of men and women are treated or, at least, illustrated in many other examples of short prose in this study (the alarmingly dysfunctional picture drawn by Siarhiej Kalienda, for instance), but several pieces by relatively young writers treat the themes of ageing and death with in some cases great sensitivity. Also worth mentioning are four of the stories in Aliaksiej Palačanski's *Moj ćvik* (My nail),[7] which introduce older people. using rich language in detailed descriptions of both people and places, In the first of them, 'Pamiž daroh' (Between paths, 2011), he depicts a dissatisfied but far from depressed old man who has an indefinite feeling that he is guilty of something in the past. His life has been made entirely rational, but at twilight he meets a young man whom he suspects of being just like his young self (Palačanski, 7). The young man eventually returns and seems quite confident, before eventually setting out for the railway station. The old man follows his new friend. but the young man is hit by a train, and the old man returns home and prosaically sets about erecting a new fence (Palačanski, 12). In another story, 'Dva Romana' (The two Ramans, 2011) a pair of old friends of different characters but with the same name discuss a plague of youths who are terrorizing their village. After the older of the Ramans has departed, the other Raman reminisces with his wife about their youthful plans of travel, but during the night, hearing the noise of breaking glass, he discovers that it is his friend (Palačanski, 19); together they run to a vandalized house and throw a sign they find there through the window of the village elder. Looking at the moon, they shout that it looks just like a cheese. Having recently decided how different they are from the hooligans, it turns out that are just like them. The moon follows them grinning at the joke:

> З дзікім гіканнем несліся дзяды па пустой вуліцы, а жоўты кавалак сыру бег за імі і смачна пасміхаўся. (Palačanski, 21)
>
> (With wild whoops the old men rushed down the empty street, and the yellow piece of cheese ran after them, smiling gleefully.)

The third story, 'Daliokija ahni' (Distant lights, 2012) is a rather touching tale of an old man, Anatoĺ, becoming disorientated at night. He imagines that his friend, Aŭhien, has become a star in the sky (Palačanski, 43) and imagines everyone in contact and enjoying themselves. Setting out towards the lights, he becomes lost and confused, settling into a long, final dream about the past (Palačanski, 47–78). At the end of the story, Aŭhien is depicted as sitting on his porch looking at the shooting stars and thinking that it would not be bad to become one of them. The last of Palačanski's stories about ageing and death is 'Dvoje' (Two of them), which describes two old men lying in bed (possibly in a hospital), listening to a storm raging outside, and wondering about life and how much of it remains for them (Palačanski, 65–66).

Quite different from the other stories mentioned in this chapter is a well-written and touching piece of family history by Natalka Charytaniuk (b. 1984) 'Furmanka śviatoha Mikoly: Siamiejnyja ŭspaminy pra sustreču sa śviatym Mikolam na darozie miž Bieraściem i Vysokim uzimku 1941 hodu'[8] (The wagon of St Mikola [Nicholas]: Family reminiscences about a meeting with St Mikola on the road between Bieraście and Vysokaje in the winter of 1941). The story is set in the time of the narrator's grandfather, although the road north from Bieraście between two rivers is still magical, and a vivid picture is given of the region's flora and fauna, including forests and storks; the slow pace of the rivers allow the inhabitants of the region to think calmly about life and death (Charytaniuk, 239). The old man has cancer, but his son Mikola, a trucker in Hamburg, cannot return in time. On his last day he seems to hear the sound of his horse and the wheels, recalling how during the war he had saved and hidden Jews on his name-day (Charytaniuk, 244), but he falls into sleep to the almost magical sound of the wheels. The narrator knows that she must end the story without using the word 'death', and tries to imagine his thoughts as she waits for the son Mikola and the Saint to come. The whole family were always in motion. As the chronicler of this time and place, she asserts that all journeys begin with the wind (Charytaniuk, 247). Unfortunately the narrative is such a continuum that it does not lend itself to quotation in small excerpts.

Quite different, but also concerning the last days of a life is 'Zvyčaj' (Custom) by Uladzimir Sadoŭski (b. 1987),[9] a rather touching story that illustrates the rural custom by which the youngest grandson takes his grandfather on his last journey, in this case back to 'sunny Miensk' the place of the old man's happiest memories.

There is no sentiment or compassion in Kalienda's 'Ehacentryst' (The egoist), which describes an old man in an untidy room making dispassionate notes about various modern horrors, including terrorist acts, from one of which he himself eventually dies. Sudden death is also depicted in 'Taŭstuha' (Fatty) by Marharyta Aliaškievič, who is also a critic and poet.[10] Two characters, Ahata (23) and Jana (16)[11] attempt to become models, but the latter feels herself to be too fat and they quarrel. After peace has finally been restored, Ahata falls out of a bus and Jana, having thought how to hide the corpse, continues to ponder her diet (Aliaškievič, 30). A less violent, but no less unpleasant aspect of death is described in 'Čužoje žyćcio' (Another's life) by Anastasija Kaciurhina (b. 1992),[12] author of two books of verse, where many of the poems are concerned with pain and anguish. A young mother, Maša, who has lost her daughter in a car accident is in a feverish state in a secure hospital, unable to comprehend how such an angel could die. Her own mother, on the other hand, is furious that her daughter cannot get over the death and wishes that Maša herself had died in the accident.

Finally may be mentioned probably the most philosophical of all the treatments of death, *Hliniany čalaviek* (Man of clay) by Aliaksiej Čubat (b. 1979), in which humans are all described as short-lived clay; he also offers some thoughts on the supremacy or otherwise of women, but, for this writer, people of both sexes and in all walks of life are merely clay, which they themselves must fashion.[13]

* * * * *

2. Fish, Animals and Birds

Fish

In one of the epigraphs to this chapter, Edgar in *King Lear* remarks that 'the fishermen that walk upon the beach / Appear like mice.'[14] There are no mice in this section, but fishing is no joking matter,[15] indeed, it rather seems to be a matter of obsession for the narrator of the book *Taŭścila i liešč* (The fat man and the bream, 2015) by Andrej Adamovič (b. 1973).[16] The plot is simple: Maksim and his friends (Viktar and Tkač) go on a fishing trip fuelled by drinking and philosophical discussions, and driven by Maksim's wife's prayers and threats that he need not come back without the desired catch (Adamovič, 72). Inevitably this description of obsession with catching a fish brings to mind other accounts of such determination, most famously Ernest Hemingway's best-known short novel, but also an excellent recent novel by Joanne Harris.[17] In several ways Adamovič's work is less deep, although the range of subjects it covers belies the assertion that it was written very quickly (26 October to 6 November) during a scholarship visit to Viĺnia (Adamovič, 98). His book uses rather difficult language (not only specific fishing terms and not including the swearing) but it is readable and interesting in its details of the group's journey and the surroundings of their place for fishing, as well as accounts of the background of the three friends, particularly Maksim. There is more about his obsession and also about his concern with philosophical ideas not all of which are shared by his companions. There are also frequent dreams and memories of the (eighty-eight) previous attempts to catch the fish, as well as his unhappy earlier life, being sacked for not getting on with colleagues in his youth. In the book he appears to vacillate between denying a real interest in fishing and thinking he has found an occupation which will make him a real man (Adamovič, 88). Death figures in the story quite extensively, both in Maksim's imaginary conversation with his son, and also earlier reflections on the subject, which fail to interest the other fishermen, who nonetheless seem at times to be quite interested in philosophy. A short example of Maksim's view is:

> Няма ў сьмерці сэнсу... Прыкрасць, што ні на чым не грунтуецца і не мае ніякага апраўдання — ні боскага, ні чалавечага (Adamovič, 84)
>
> (There is no sense in death... A disgusting thing that is not based on anything and which has no justification — neither divine nor human)

Important elements in the story are a car crash that the trio pass on their way, with dead children, and also a scene they witness of a child being bullied. Amidst all the men's talking and drinking, they return to discussion of these scenes as the story progresses. Also important, although not part of the trip, is Maksim's wife who appears to be the dominant partner in their marriage. At the end, however, after Maksim has been sick over the fish, apparently reviving it, he seems to assert himself rather bathetically (Adamovič, 98). *Taŭścila i liešč* is, however long it took to write, a far from insignificant debut in prose.

A small bream also appears in the debut novel of Siarhiej Kalienda, which is mostly about the introspective trials and tribulations of young people, but which also includes a miniature, 'Ryby' (Fish, 2009), in which the narrator imagines himself as a fish swimming too far for safety, and in his alcohol-induced dreamlike state being advised by a little fish to be more sensible, as all fish long to become people, whilst the narrator, struggling drunkenly in the water, tells the little bream that there would be nothing for it to do amongst humans (Kalienda, 181–82). More characteristic of the poisoned world described by this writer is the long short story, 'Novy dom' (The new house, 2006), about an ill-matched, rather mercenary young couple trying to move into a new house. Their little boy goes to a pool on the building site, looking for fish, but falls in and drowns (Kalienda, 110–11). His death becomes a catalyst for guilty paranoia and reproaches from the wife of the husband for his not lamenting the death of their child enough (Kalienda, 119), after which he dreams of his own childhood and of drowning in a puddle (Kalienda, 120–21). The pair finally split up.

Two more writers deserve brief mention here. 'Žyvaja ryba' (A live fish, 2016) is an early story by Maryja Maliaŭka, who was born in Kyiv in 1990 and now lives in Miensk.[18] It is mainly a plea for crippled and otherwise disabled people to be able to go out into the world and not just sit at home. The purchase of a live carp, however, makes the narrator sick, and has a comparable effect on her tyrannical brother (who is also angry about his mother's tumour). The fish in this story is a catalyst for paranoia and unhappiness, but it is the blind friend with cerebral palsy who is at the centre of the work. Even more tangential to the theme of fish is 'Čužoje hniazdo'(An alien nest, 2001) by Paŭlina Kačatkova,[19] in which she debates various sizes of aquariums, recalling a very small earlier one and being criticized by a poet for her lack of spiritual values, apparently confusing *som* (catfish) and *slon* (elephant) (Kačatkova, 140). The narrator also has thoughts on parrots that do or do not speak and on dog collars, not to mention a married suitor, so this is hardly a story about fish.

Animals

Amongst animals in the texts under review the most frequent animal is, perhaps predictably, a dog (known in England as a man's best friend), although this animal appears relatively rarely in young Belarusian prose. Paŭlina Kačatkova in her story, 'Pra adnu kabietu' (About one woman) describes a dog as a hundred times cleverer than a person. The woman of the title, Jadwiga, lives in isolation at the top of a hill, not noticing the various changes of political power and so on below her. She lives with her beloved dog, Ren, which, when she dies, just wails and will not leave the house. The priest, however, refuses to give her a Christian burial because it was rumoured, absurdly, that she had 'lived with' a dog (Kačatkova, 135–43 [136–37]). Kalienda follows Hamlet in 'Huĺnia ŭ inteliekt' (Intellectual play) where he ponders the question of why man is superior to the rest of nature, concluding that it is all lies, and that human life is nothing more than a chain of suffering (Kalienda, 65). He does, however, also offer a canine point of view on the question:

> Не вытрымаўшы суровага маўчання гаспадара і адсутнасці звыклай дынамікі ў целе, загаварыў Сабака, які увесь час адпачываў пад сталом, 'Я зусім нядаўна гартаў Бержэрака, трэба даць яго кніжку табе пачытаць! Ты павінны азнаёміцца з гэтым мудрацом ад Быцця. Гэтым геніем, сынам Месяца і Бясконнасці!' — думаў Сабака. Яму вельмі карцела дапамагчы.
>
> [...]
>
> Абыякавасць да ўсяго жывога — заметная рыса чалавека! Ён гаспадар! Але хто яму сказаў пра гэта?! (Kalienda, 64–65)
>
> (Unable to bear the severe silence of the master and the absence of his usual physical exercise, the Dog, who had all the time been resting under the table, thought, 'I very recently leafed through the book of Bergerac, and I must give you his little book to read! You should get to know this wise man from Existence. This genius, son of the Moon and Infinity. He greatly longed to help. [...] Indifference to all living things is a notable feature of man! He is the master! But who told him about that?!)

A variety of dogs appear in two debut stories by Hanna Šybut: in 'Śviatlo i ciemra' (Light and dark) wild dogs come to a village. In 'Samy liepšy tata ŭ śviece' (The best father in the world) the hung-over male narrator who has been turned out of his home is further enraged by new neighbours who have brought noisy dogs with them; it turns out that their house is being made into a refuge for abandoned animals. Eventually, he realizes that people frequently treat animals badly, and that animals are often cleverer, and certainly, kinder than people. When he returns home with a kitten for his daughter and is forgiven by his wife, the girl says, 'Татачка... Ты самы добры тата ў свеце!' (Daddy... You are the kindest dad in the world!). The ending of this decidedly sentimental piece is appropriate: 'Як лёгка, аказваецца, зрабіць добрае, як лёгка і як важна!' (How easy it turns out to be to do good, and how easy it is and how important!) (Šybut, 331–32).

The other references to cats in young Belarusian prose seem to be loosely related to eroticism. For instance, 'Chlopčyk na lyžach' (The boy on skis) by Aliona Bielanožka (b. 1985)[20] describes the eponymous boy, Dzianiska, in a round glass ornament that the cat Rysia rolls around the flat before they both fall from the balcony into a snowdrift. The girl whose ball it is seems to meet a man called Dzianis who invites her for coffee, but suddenly Rysia returns with the ball. Quite different is Sieviaryn Kviatkoŭski's '"Zdrastvuj, Vasia..."' ('Hello, Vasia...') in which a writer produces jingles about his pet cat that appear in internet publications as 'Vieršy pra Vaśku' (Poems about Vaśka). One example will suffice:

> У адным сяле, ня важна дзе,
> Хадзіў Васёк па магазіну.
> Ён піва піў, еў мармэляд
> І марыў трахнуць цёцю Зіну. (Kviatkoŭski, 45)
>
> (In one village, no matter where,
> Vasiok went to a shop,
> He drank beer, ate jam
> And dreamed of screwing Aunty Zina.)

Appropriately enough at the end of the story, after a New Year's party the writer has an erotic dream, and he notes, 'Thank you Vasia!' (Kviatkoŭski, 50).

A short story by Taćciana Barysik (b. 1977) (from a selection, 'Kachańnie ŭ našym kuście' (Love in our group),[21] 'Pra liuboŭ i "Družbu"' (About love and 'Friendship') is about a man and his beloved cow Maliutka. It begins in the style of a fairy tale, but the friendship is broken when the head of the local collective farm digs up the cow's pasture and buys the cow for meat, then with the money buys a power-saw for his farm. Here is the opening:

> За трыма лясамі, за трыма ўзгоркамі й трыма канавамі на ўскрайку нявялічкай вёсачкі жыў чалавек. І была ў яго карова зь мянушкай Малюта. Чалавек вельмі любіў сваю карову, й ганарыўся ёю. (Barysik, 63)
>
> (Beyond three forests, beyond three hillocks and three ditches at the end of a tiny village lived a man. And he had a cow named Maliutka. The man loved his cow very much and took great pride in it.)

Finally may be mentioned the only mammal capable of sustained flight, the bat. In a short story of 2005 by Arciom Kavalieŭski, 'Kažanicha' (The bat), the eponymous animal narrates how having had her sounds recorded she suddenly finds herself a pop star. The main themes of the story are the relationship between the bat and humans, as well as partners and loneliness. In this respect, although we are presented with the bat's point of view, the theme of a relationship between animals and humans is present, even in the case of what many regard as a sinister creature.

* * * * *

Birds

Before examining any texts, it may be mentioned that Maryja Roŭda's book, *Kliničny vypadak, aĺbo Daremnyja ucioki* has a particularly threatening black bird on the surrealist cover designed by Uladzimir Dryndrožyk. Nasta Mancevič, who of course called her first book *Ptuški* (Birds), seems undoubtedly to regard the feathered creatures as part of a hostile and threatening environment. Quite different is Marharyta Latyškievič (b. 1989), one of the best contributors to the anthology of debut compositions, *Moj dzień pačynajecca*, who has a good command of dialogue and narration, although she is occasionally a bit wordy. Her early stories combine elements of historical fantasy and science fiction, but, from her cycle of stories 'a-550-1', 'Tumannaść miortvaj halavy' (Mistiness of a dead head)[22] ends with the narrator imagining Belarus's national bird:

> І я ведаю: калі дабрацца да вяршыні і зірнуць уніз, можна будзе пабачыць белых буслаў з чырвонымі дзюбамі, буслаў, якія ідуць па траве, высока падымаючы нагі. (Latyškievič, 155)

> (And I know that if I reach the peak and look down, I shall be able to see white storks with red beaks, storks which walk through the grass raising high their legs.)

Paŭlina Kačatkova's heroine in 'Čužoje hniazdo' only demanded of a parrot that it could speak, but Valieryja Sarotnik (b. 1988) in one of her 'Vosiem kazak dlia daroslych' (Seven fairy tales for grownups), 'Pra jablyki' (About apples),[23] describes a brilliant young scientist who continually invents useless things, as his only friend, a parrot, keeps telling him. Even when he seems to achieve success his euphoria is contrasted by the far calmer wise parrot:

> Толькі трэба дапамагчы яму навучыцца думаць.
> Дзеля такога можна выцерпець якую заўгодна лаянку. (Sarotnik, 264)

> (I must just help him to learn to think.
> For that one could put up with any amount of cursing.)

As a coda to the genre of fairy tales, the inventively witty Anka Upala ends her tale 'Balachon Balachonavič i Zlaja Bavioryca' (Balachon Balachonavič and the Evil Squirrel) with the following sentiment:

> Хто казку слухаў — патыліцу чухаў, хто казку прачытаў — той дзяржаўнага розуму чалавек. (Upala, 34)
>
> (Who listened to a fairy story scratched the back of their head, who read a fairy story is a person with an official cast of mind.)

It may also be mentioned here that Upala also has several stories about insects, including 'Ylk' and 'Prusačnaja vajna' (War of the cockroaches) (Upala, 56–58, 76–77), as well as a gold fish that wants gold teeth (Upala, 6) and a cat with the absurd name of Chonavantura, that has relatives in Warsaw, but refuses to answer their telephone calls (Upala, 7).

* * * * *

Such notes of absurdity that end this chapter take no account of the pathos, even tragedy and other serious concerns that accompany the humour, but it is nevertheless a far from insignificant element in the response to the human condition as well as the animal world presented by the writers represented here.

Notes to Chapter 2

1. William Shakespeare, *As You Like It*, II, vii, 163–66.
2. Aliaksiej Palačanski, *Moj ćvik* (Minsk: Halijafy, 2014) (hereafter Palačanski), pp. 98–106.
3. Alieś Byčkoŭski, 'Žnička', *Horad za 101-m kilamietram* (Minsk: Lohvinaŭ, 2004) (hereafter Byčkoŭski), pp. 86–88 (p. 86).
4. Anatoĺ Ivaščanka, 'Pach voli', *Anatalohija* (Minsk: Knihazbor, 2015) (hereafter Ivaščanka, *Anatalohija*), pp. 5–10. The title, incidentally, appears to be a combination of anatomy and anthology, a word that does not otherwise exist in English or Belarusian.
5. Jaŭhien Martynovič, 'Siem rečaŭ, jakija ja nie budu rabić, kali vyrastu! List u budučniu', *Mdp*, pp. 199–201.
6. Kryścina Banduryna, 'Śliady na čystaj papiery', *Mdp* (hereafter Banduryna), pp. 29–32.
7. Aliaksiej Palačanski, *Moj ćvik* (Minsk: Halijafy, 2014) (hereafter Palačanski).
8. Natalka Charytaniuk. 'Furmanka śviatoha Mikoly: Siamiejnyja ŭspaminy pra sustreču sa śviatym Mikolam na darozie miž Bieraściem i Vysokim uzimku 1941 hodu' (hereafter Charytaniuk), *Žvzpk*, pp. 237–47.
9. Uladzimir Sadoŭski, 'Zvyčaj', *Mdp*, pp. 253–56 (hereafter Sadoŭski).
10. Marharyta Aliaškievič, 'Taŭstuha' in *Ptuški liohkich pavodzinaŭ*, comp. by A. Chadanovič (Minsk: Lohvinaŭ, 2013) (hereafter *Plp*), pp. 23–30 (hereafter Aliaškievič).
11. The same characters also appear in another story 'Staniki' (Bras), which is somewhat reminiscent of chick lit.
12. Anastasija Kaciurhina, 'Čužoje žyćcio', *Mdp*, pp. 128–29.

13. Aliaksiej Čubat, *Hliniany čalaviek* (Minsk: Halijafy, 2008), pp. 27–28.
14. William Shakespeare, *King Lear*, IV, vi, 17–18.
15. In Edgar's speech there are some bawdy jokes later in the quoted passage.
16. Andrej Adamovič, *Taŭścila i lieśč* (Minsk: Lohvinaŭ, 2015) (hereafter Adamovič). This book won a prize, as did Adamovič's first book of verse: *Dzień paezii śmierci dzień* (Minsk: Lohvinaŭ, 2012). Fishing as a recreation was probably introduced by Izaac Walton, the first edition of whose *The Compleat Angler* was published in London by Richard Marriot of St Dunstan-in-the-West in 1653.
17. Ernest Hemingway's prize-winning short novel, *The Old Man and the Sea* (1952) described a desperate battle to catch a large marlin in the Straits of Florida. Joanne Harris's deep and grim wartime novel *Five Quarters of the Orange* (2001) features Old Mother of the murky waters of the Loire in which there lurks a terrible quasi-mythical old river pike.
18. Maryja Maliaŭka, 'Žyvaja ryba', *Dziejasloŭ*, 2 (81) (2006), 188–92 (hereafter Maliaŭka).
19. Paŭlina Kačatkova, 'Čužoje hniazdo', *Žvzpk*, pp. 139–43 (hereafter Kačatkova).
20. Aliona Bielanožka, 'Chlopčyk na lyžach', *Mdp*, pp. 39–42.
21. Taciana Barysik, 'Kachańnie ŭ našym kuście', *Žvzpk*, pp. 58–64.
22. Marharyta Latyškievič, 'Tumannaść miortvaj halavy', *Mdp*, pp. 148–55 (hereafter Latyškievič).
23. Valieryja Sarotnik, 'Vosiem kazak dlia daroslych', *Mdp*, pp. 260–68 (hereafter Sarotnik).

CHAPTER 3

Religion, Superstition, Philosophy and Fantasy

Shakespeare, 'When I pray and think, I think and pray
To several subjects'
Measure for Measure, II, iv, 1–2

The three categories of this section are not as remote (at least to English eyes) as they might at first seem. W.R. Inge, Dean of St Pauls and Professor of Divinity at Cambridge suggested that 'to become a popular religion, it is only necessary for a superstition to enslave a philosophy.'[1] On the other hand, Benedetto Croce, even more provocatively, held that 'philosophy removes from religion all reason for existing.'[2]

Religion

In *Spring Shoots*[3] there were a number of young poets in whose work religion was a topic (mostly Catholic or Uniate, sometimes unspecified). Orthodoxy is the officially approved confession, it may be thought, particularly because it is the main one in Russia. Against this background, particularly striking was a poem by Anatoĺ Ivaščanka, 'Vierš niesvabody' (A poem of unfreedom) in which he comments on friends' attitude to his Orthodoxy:[4]

перад сном
хтосьці скажа, што ад майго праваслаўя
добра патыхае забабонамі...'. (*SS*, 71) [5]

(before sleep / somebody will say that from my Orthodoxy / there is a strong stink of superstition...)

By contrast, religion is not a frequent theme in young prose, and some of the examples mentioned here display something less than piety. For instance, in 'Dziakuj' (Thank you) (*Mdp*, 349–52) by Paval Jakuć (b. 1993), the narrator aspires to become a saint and, as a first step, on strong conviction, goes to Poland to train for the priesthood. On his return to Belarus at Christmas he meets a girl, Jasia, whom he had loved when he was fifteen but whom he has not seen for six months, He cannot forget his love and they have sex, which radically changes his life. Nonetheless, he returns to Poland, planning to devote his whole life to God. Eight years later, returning to Belarus to work in a new church, he finds himself conducting a wedding service for Jasia, who asks him whether it is alright that she has a child (clearly his). Overcome by fear and remorse, he goes to the river and sorrowfully kneels down, when suddenly he hears the sound of Jasia's little girl drowning. After managing to save her, he himself drowns, thanking God for everything. The irony of this plot-rich story is a far cry from the apparently heartfelt exclamations of faith by some young poets.

More cynicism than naivety is reflected in a piece by essayist, poet and translator Tania Skarynkina (b. 1969), 'Boža moj' (My God),[6] in which the young narrator's aunt is threatened by a priest that if she does not make her niece pray she will incur a great sin. The girl tries to do her best and is christened at age 18 by answering correctly two questions about the English language. She wishes it had all happened earlier — for the beautiful ceremony. Now she prays with her eyes shut.

Also sceptical if not cynical is Kalienda's 'Kryvadušnik' (The hypocrite) (Kalienda, 99–105) in which a young man goes into church to confess to the sins of his grandfather who had raped a young girl; he is followed by a stranger who also appears anxious to confess the sins of his recently deceased grandfather who had also raped and participated in the gang rape of a young girl. The priest, receiving these confessions, realizes that he was a friend of the rapist in the first part of the story, and what a hypocrite he is (Kalienda, 105).

Finally, in Kaściukievič's 'Bieteĺhiejzijanskija chroniki' (The Betelgeuse chronicles) we read about the new religion of (particularly foreign) car ownership:

> Хрысціянскія сьвятары, мусульманскія мулы, юдэйскія рабіны і будысцкія манахі ўдзень яшчэ мусолілі свае літургіі, але ўжо адвячоркам шчыравалі напоўніцу — перабудоўвалі бажніцы пад гаражы. (Kaściukievič, 107)
>
> (Christian priests, Muslim mullahs, Jewish rabbis and Buddhist monks by day fingered the pages of their liturgies, but at the coming of evening put their hearts into rebuilding their places of worship in the style of garages.)

Superstition

References to what might be called superstitions occur from time to time in young prose, particularly, but not only, in works concerned with rural life. In 'Navina dnia' (The day's news) by Taćciana Barysik, a pensioner, Liuba, regrets her lack of mobility but appreciates visitors who come and bring her news (Barysik, 65). One day there has been special news and she goes to her friend Savončycha to pass it on, as the matter is too important for them to put on television. It is not, however, the 'miracle' (*dziva*) of a whirlwind damaging bales of hay (albeit described in colourful rural language), but the discussions that follow that give the story colour. A teacher of physics, for instance, has suggested that it is a change of atmospheric pressure but this does not entirely satisfy Liuba:

> Можа, вы і правільна кажаце пра ціск гэты. Толькі калі у той віхор нож кінуць, дык кроў зьявіцца, бо ведзьма! (Barysik, 67)
>
> (Maybe you're even right talking about this pressure. But if you throw a knife into that whirlwind, then blood will appear, for it's a witch!)

Savončycha, for her part, recalls terrifying sights in the graveyard, with a twisting pillar of phosphorus rising from a twinkling fire inside a coffin and how it is important to hold your breath or it will come and smother you (Barysik, 67). Liuba rushes home in a panic, whilst somewhere over the horizon sputniks are being sent into space and the battle against terrorism continues (Barysik, 68).[7]

Kryścina Kurčankova's 'Što-koĺviečy pra haradskich eĺfaŭ' (A little about urban elves)[8] describes the lives of elves and ghosts but also has elements of religion: the icons appear fresh and alive in church (Kurčankova, 147), and a quasi-excerpt from a prayer printed in bold seems to have some relationship to it: '***верую памажы майму нявер'ю***' (*Žvzpk*, 151) (***I believe help me in my unbelief***). It may be remembered that the German husband of the unhappy narrator in Maryja Roŭda's 'Kliničny vypadak, albo Daremnyja ŭcioki' is referred to as a gnome (Roŭda, *passim*).

Philosophy and Abstract Thought

Philosophy and thought are close cousins, and the suggestion by Alieś Jemialianaŭ-Šylovič (b. 1987) that 'freedom is stability' certainly qualifies as thought but not philosophy as such:[9] in 'Svaboda' (Freedom) he writes: 'Свабода — элементарнае (ня)веданне таго, што ты несвабодны' (Jemialianaŭ, 61) (Freedom is the elementary [lack of] knowledge that you are not free). At the end he expands the definition by saying: 'я атаясамліваю свабоду са стабільнасцю' (Jemialianaŭ, 61) (I equate freedom with stability).[10]

A comparable abstract reflection opens Bajarovič's *Šali* where he suggests that 'атрымоўваецца, што нашае жыццё пабудавана на процілегласцях' (Bajarovič, 11) (it turns out that our life is built on contradictions); the scales of the title are what balance the two extremes. He continues this thought at the end of one of his other miniatures, 'jadnańnie' (unity): 'І чамусьці здаецца, што ў гэтым свеце ўжо ніколі не будзе яднання' (Bajarovič, 14) (And for some reason it seems that in our world there will never more be unity). Another thought is expressed in 'chluśnia' (lying), in which an elaborate build-up is followed by the thought in the last line that if there were no lying, there would not be any genuine people (Bajarovič, 32–33).

There are several references to well-known philosophers, particularly of the twentieth century, in texts where they may hardly have been expected. For instance, in Andrej Adamovič's *Taŭśila i lieść* Maksim, having failed to interest his fishing companions with his ideas about death (see Chapter 2), provokes one of the others, Vicia, to advise him to come out of his existential crisis, referring to Jean-Paul Sartre and Søren Kierkegaard (Adamovič, 86). In Kalienda's 'Vanity' (Vomiting) the unattractive main character is called Danila Lakanaü (Kalienda, 11 et ff) — even the iconoclastic Jacques Lacan might have taken exception to this reference. The mention of Dale Carnegie in another story, 'Klub' (The club) (Kalienda, 84), is stretching the already elastic concept of philosophy too far.[11]

* * * * *

Fantasy

Fantasy in various forms has been and will be mentioned in various other chapters. It is also connected with science fiction and dreams, at least as much as it is related to religion, although many unbelievers do indeed regard religious faith as fantasy. What follows is a survey of some of the fantastic elements in young prose that, for good reason, have not found a place elsewhere.

To begin with an imaginative example of an historical fantasy already mentioned in Chapter 1, 'Paliavańnie na pačvarnaha parsiuka', from *Imia hrušy* by Siarhiej Balachonaŭ, where there are many rumours and superstitions throughout the story. The following excerpt illustrates this phenomenon well:

> Між тым на месьсце віленскім пагудка прабегла, дзей у адным з хлявоў мяшчанскіх сьвіньня ў прыплодзе прынесла нейкую бэстыю, пачвару заістую. Ніхто не ведаў, што рабіці з вырадкам. Быў ён большым ад іншых парсюкоў ды меў, як казалі кніжнікі, пілігрымы й купцы, голаў малпы, цібо абізяны — зьвера, што вадзіўся ў старане індыянскай і ў далёкіх крэсах афрыцкіх. (Balachonaŭ, 143)
>
> (Meanwhile a rumour ran through the city of Vilnia that in one of the burghers' styes a pregnant pig had brought forth some kind of beast, a real monster. Nobody knew what to do with this deformed creature. He was bigger than other boars, and had, according to what scholars, pilgrims and merchants said, the head of some monkey or ape, a beast to be found in the Indian land and in distant African regions.)

Quite different is the work of Paval Kaściukievič where fantastic events abound in the modern world. In 'Šestsot šeśćdziesiat šeść viečaroŭ' (Six hundred and sixty-six evenings), for instance, Satan pays a visit to Miensk, but as events progress it turns out that it is all happening in the narrator's head, so that for the first time in 666 evenings he was not thinking about his girlfriend Śvieta. As in all this writer's work, however, it is the narrative detail that delights: for instance. a couple whose romantic plans are ruined, and a hooligan who tries to out-swear the birds, as a result of which his lips turn white like a beak, whilst the rest of his face also becomes white (Kaściukievič, 28–31) (p. 30). Before turning to more of this writer's fantastic stories, it is worth mentioning a piece by Anatoĺ Ivaščanka, 'Fliejta Daždžu' (Rain's flute) (Ivaščanka, *Anatalohija*, 49–55) which also seems to echo faintly Mikhail Bulgakov's brilliant and much-censored novel about the devil visiting Moscow, *Master i Margarita* (Master and Margarita) (1928–1940). Ivaščanka's story is marred by an (over-)elaborate opening and excessive literariness, such as constant direct addresses to the reader and many complications. It does, however, relate a lively concatenation of events that lead to unhappiness and disaster (Ivaščanka, *Anatalohija*, 55). Returning to Kaściukievič, his 'Vajna z dmuchaŭcami' (War with dandelions) is set at a meeting of the World Congress of Belarusianists in Miensk, when a sudden shout of 'War, war!' causes uproar and much panic among the public, including fears of the apocalypse, rather like the situation in the same author's 'Suka-krot', which will be discussed in Chapter 4. The dandelion invasion centres on the Jewish section of the congress where Marc Chagall was the centre of attention, but, doubtless self-indulgently, I should like to quote a brief and utterly improbable discussion between two foreign scholars interested in Belarus but who have never met; in the present writer's case it is a case of the proverbial 'fame at last':

> 'Я не хачу паміраць, я такі малады і таленавіты, у мяне студэнты, навуковы працэс без мяне не пойдзе!' — раптам крык. Пазнаём голас прафесара, знаўцы слуцкіх паясоў, Цімаці Шнайдэра.
>
> 'Пойдзе, не баісь', цэдзіць у адказ знаўца беларускай літаратуры, прафесар Арнольд Макмілер [*sic*].
>
> 'Нашто я пайшоў да беларусістаў?... Мяне ж запрасілі на з'езд паланістаў ў Літавэл і літуаністаў у Палангу...'
>
> 'Будь мужыком, вазьмі "калаш" у рукі', злавесна шэпча знаўца белліту.
>
> 'Але ў нас іншая зброя — М-16, надзейная вінтоўка амерыканскай пяхоты... Я хачу М-16!..'
>
> [...]
>
> 'І калі трэба, памрэш, сабака, за беларускую літаратуру.'
>
> 'There is nothing to die for!'
>
> 'You told me!' (Kaściukievič, 51–52)
>
> ('I do not want to die, I am so young and talented, I have students, the scholarly process will not move forward without me!' — comes a sudden cry. We recognize the voice of Professor Timothy Snyder.

'It will progress, do not fear', replies through clenched teeth, the specialist in Belarusian literature Professor Arnold McMiler [*sic.*]

'Why did I come to the Belarusianists? After all I was invited to a congress of Polonists in Litowel and of Lithuanianists in Palanga...'

'Be a man and take a "kalash" in your hands', whispers the specialist in Bellit ominously.

'But we have a different weapon, the M-16, the reliable rifle of American infantrymen... I want an M-16!...

[...]

'And if you have to, you'll die like a dog for Belarusian literature.'

'There is nothing to die for!'

'You told me!')[12] (Kaściukievič, 51–52)

This lively romp ends with a quotation from Adam Adamovič's poem, 'Italijcy' (The Italians). Other fantastic and inventive stories by Kaściukievič include 'Kliatyja 1990-ja' (The accursed 1990s), which depicts a time of total chaos, in which imaginary fantasies flourish (Kaściukievič, 91–95) and the book's title story 'Zbornaja RB pa niehaloŭnych vidach sportu' (The national team of the Belarusian Republic for minor types of sport) in which are described with entertaining gusto a number of fantastic sports (Kaściukievič, 122–25). Some other stories closer to science fiction will be discussed later.

The already mentioned young writer Valeryja Sarotnik has several fantastic stories in her 'Vosiem kazak dlia daroslych'. Apart from personified trees and toads (not to mention fairies), she also gives life to trams. For example, in 'Pra tramvaj' (About a tram) the eponymous vehicle dreams of being a train going to exotic places and not just in circles around the city (Sarotnik, 260–61); the author notes provocatively that humans also follow rails in their lives. In 'Mary ździaśniajucca' (Dreams come true) a fairy grants a tram's wish to be a train, but the tram unexpectedly refuses, later wondering whether it should have accepted (Sarotnik, 264–65). 'Žyć niby ŭ kazcy' (To live as in a fairy story) is somewhat convoluted, ending with words that might apply to several of the earlier stories also: 'Усё можа быць. Але людзі ў наш час не ведаюць, чаго хочаць.' (Sarotnik, 265–68) (268) (Everything is possible. But in our time people do not know what they want.)

Two of Aliona Bielanožka's stories combine fantasy with mild satire. In 'Maladzik pa niebie chodzić' (The new moon crosses the sky), for instance, she describes a spaceship as a military item that is supposed to destroy itself rather than surrender. After various episodes satirizing military discipline, it lands on earth harmlessly.[13] In 'Dzicia ziamli' (Child of the earth) Icarus and Leda decide to have a child and go to a well-guarded genetics centre. The various options they are offered allow the author some satirical observations on genetic planning (Bielanožka, 59–64). Quite different is a complex story, 'Hrebień u skryni' (The cockscomb in a chest), which describes the murderous search of a mermaid for revenge, following the loss of her metal comb (Bielanožka, 42–48).

Violence of various (particularly mechanical) kinds is more characteristic of the stories of Aleś Byčkoŭski. For example, in 'Zlaviesnaja ruža štučnaha kachańnia' (The sinister rose of artificial love) (Byčkoŭski, 77–84) a student of cybernetics, Lika, is in love with a hacker Jan, although the relationship is not warm. Jan compares God's creation of the world to Man's creation of the computer (Byčkoŭski, 81); they are both completely engaged in the study of artificial intelligence, and Lika proposes introducing the computer to Margaret Mitchell's novel, *Gone with the Wind*, in the hope that it may write a sequel (Byčkoŭski, 82). Suddenly, however, a huge explosion throws Lika out of the window where she sees a huge metallic rose with poisonous spikes, and in the middle of this monster lies a photo of Lika herself (Byčkoŭski, 84). Very different is another of his stories, 'Naščadki nieŭraŭ' (Bearers of the werewolf gene) (89–116), in which the two characters are a young girl Nasta and a policeman Vadzim, who at the beginning of the story believes that all werewolves were killed in World War II (Byčkoŭski, 107). After various mysterious and alarming adventures, it turns out that both of them carry the werewolf gene and that neither of them, particularly Nasta, can ever have a normal life again. In this connection it may be worth mentioning that Anatoĺ Ivaščanka in one of his poems, 'na sieansie ekzarcyzmu' (at a séance of exorcism), sees one of his features as being that of a werewolf (*vaŭkalak*).[14]

Marharyta Latyškievič speculates about an ancient dragon in 'Kali ich nie zastaniecca' (When none of them will be left) (Latyškievič, 146–47). Three other stories in 'a-530-1 (cykl apaviadańniaŭ)' (a-530-1 [a cycle of stories]) feature the same characters, and may be said to present science fiction with a human face. The setting is in the distant future but the characters have recognizably Belarusian features: Hlionik, presumably from another planet, Hiz, the pilot of a spaceship, and a third character who may or may not be the huge Universe with its many secrets. In one story of this cycle the already mentioned, 'Tumannaść miortvaj halavy' (The mistiness of a dead head) (Latyškievič. 148–55), some humour is to be found in the characters' concern to repair or replace a kettle. The story's viewpoint is made clear when Hlionik informs the thick-skinned, constantly smiling Hiz: 'Усе зямляне вар'яты' (Latyškievič, 154) (All earthlings are crazy). Comparable, although different in tone, is Paval Kaściukievič's story 'Amaĺ: pierajmajučy Ethara K.' (Almost: in imitation of Etgar K[eret])[15] which treats a mixture of problems of life in space interspersed with problems of interpersonal relations on earth. The clear aim is to de-mystify cosmonauts' lives as compared with the way they are shown in films; for instance, they have to appeal to earth for food and spacesuits, and make their first steps on the moon in completely unsuitable dress (Kaściukievič, 67–77). The same author's already mentioned 'Bieteĺhiejzinskija chroniki' features a robot militia-man who is only capable of investigating one person at once (Kaściukievič, 104–05) and cars that can fly through the air, even to the cosmos (Kaściukievič, 109–10).

Aliaksiej Palačanski is the author of several completely fantastic stories, of which a few examples will suffice. 'Pieĺmieni. Sudzilišča jedakoŭ' (Pelmeni. Judgment on the eaters) (Palačanski, 54–64) is a three part story in which a man refuses to eat disgusting pelmeni, but finds them constantly increasing in size (as in a grim fairy tale) and is eventually eaten by them as revenge. Palačanski is also notable for his use of richly elaborate language. One good example is his 'Na kavalki' (In pieces) where the theme is, as in Gogol''s *Nos* (The Nose, 1836), errant body parts. The following example illustrates the misery caused to its owner by his severed head:

> Мая галава каціласся і смяялася, а раззлаванае цела бегла ззаду ды слепа шнарыла на пустой шыі.
>
> Я сам лунаў дзесьці збоку, гайдаўся на хвалях ветраных настрояў і назіраў за сваёй мітуснёй. (Palačanski, 67)

> (My head rolled and laughed, and my infuriated body ran behind, blindly feeling at his empty neck.
>
> I myself was floating somewhere to the side, swinging on the waves of aerial moods, and observing my own turmoil.)

The head becomes an intellectual, and eventually takes off in a doomed spaceship. As in Gogol''s story, the main interest lies in the rich detail, for example, the comments of bystanders on a headless body, or the various medical and political discussions, as well as the head's examination by a psychologist. The latter enjoys life and even falls in love, but eventually succumbs to drink. The language is rich, and an example of Palačanski's fecund use of imagery is a description of the rake who is the head's main drinking partner: 'стольки бутэлек раскідана паўсюль, як забытыя дзеці' (Palačanski, 71) (so many bottles were scattered everywhere, like forgotten children). The last of Palačanski's stories to be mentioned here is 'U haściach' (Visiting) (Palačanski, 86–97), a tale of three people invited to dinner by a host who almost immediately disappears. The main themes are memory loss, personal insecurity, the need for leadership, stability and a definite, not amorphous, place in the world. At the end, the least confident guest finds himself in a (typically nightmarish) ever-lengthening corridor; he returns to the bathroom and on emerging immediately finds his host who is warmly inviting him to dinner (Palačanski, 97). Comparable, perhaps, is Uladzimir Sadoŭski's 'U mianie niama pačućciaŭ, alie ja pavinien kachać' (I have no feelings, but I must love) (Sadoŭski, 256–59), in which the setting moves quickly from prosaic reality to a meeting of the narrator and his gang with an old man, Erikson, who leads them into a fantastically well-equipped wartime bunker (for instance, with a hot meal set for four); the fantasy continues with the death of most of the young men, ostensibly for their banality and fickleness in love.

Paŭlina Kačatkova in 'Liasnoje' (Woodlands) writes miniatures about life on a farmstead that features not only animals, but also angels and ghosts (Kačatkova, 131–34). Her most interesting work, 'Pra adnu kabietu', was discussed in Chapter 2.

Finally may be mentioned a fantastic story by Maryja Roŭda, 'Kaliekcyjanier' (The collector) (Roŭda, 149–53), that is quite unlike other stories in the work of a writer who is usually particularly concerned with the problems of women and love. The eponymous collector, despite having felt the burden of glory from childhood (Roŭda, 149), has to remain in a large box with little men who provide amusement for ruthless and hostile giants. There are a number of other bizarre elements in this strange tale, not least that the collector walks around with a prickly conker in his pocket (Roŭda, 152).

* * * * *

Dreams are both ubiquitous and, in a sense, universal in literature. Many feature elsewhere in this book, but a few other instances may be worth mentioning. The second part of Aleś Byčkoŭski's *Horad za 101-m kilamietram* is a 'trypcich dlia barabana z arkiestram' (triptych for drum and orchestra) (Byčkoŭski, 23–74), of which each of the three parts is described as a dream. Sieviaryn Kviatkoŭski in 'Patajemnaja žadańnie' (Secret longing) describes various types of dreams, particularly of alcohol and sex. More mysterious is his 'Siniaje vakno' (The blue window) in which the hero, dreaming of a blue window across Miensk's main avenue from his work, experiences a number of unpredictable changes in his life. Finally, Jaŭhien Martynovič in 'Mora' (The sea)[16] writes of various dreams, including one of the sea, which changes and stops after he has actually seen the subject of his dream in real life (Martynovič, 202).

* * * * *

It is clear that in the preponderance of fantasy, including science fiction and dreams in this chapter, the tail has been, so to speak, wagging the dog of religion. Had, however, the fantasy preceded the section on religion, it might have been even more potentially offensive to believers than following religion by superstition. Be that as it may, the fantastic stories above are rarely less than entertaining, and remind the reader of the vivid imaginations both of the youngest Belarusian writers and of those of greater experience.

Notes to Chapter 3

1. W.R. Inge, *Outspoken Essays*, Second series (London: Longmans Green and Co, 1922), p. 163.
2. Benedetto Croce, *The Essence of Aesthetic* (1912), first published in England by William Heinemann, London 1921, I, p. 8

3. *SS*, p. 71; translated as *Ruń: Maladyja bielaruskija paety pačatku XXI stahoddzia* (Minsk: Knihazbor, 2016) (hereafter *Ruń*), p. 89.
4. Although Orthodoxy is the officially supported confession in Belarus (partly, but not only, because it is the main confession in their dominant neighbour, Russia), there are also some Catholics, but very many young poets and writers appear to adhere to Uniate beliefs.
5. Anatoĺ Ivaščanka, *Chaj tak* (Minsk: Halijafy: 2013), p. 17. An author's note to the text says that this verse was written for the project *Vierš na svabodu*. The fact that it does not appear in the volume of that name edited by Valiancina Aksak (Radio Svaboda, 2002) may be due to the macaronic swearing that follows the above quotation; the words in English imply indifference to his friends' scepticism. For a commentary on such use of English swear words, see Arnold McMillin, 'Macaronic Writing by Young Belarusian Poets: The Attraction of English "barbarisms"', *Przegląd wschodnioeuropejski*, VII/2 (2016), 197–207 (hereafter McMillin, Macaronic) (pp. 199–200).
6. Tania Skarynkina, *Šmat Česlava Milaša, krychu Elvisa Presli: Ese, napisanyja dlia 'Budźma' ŭ 2014–2015* (Minsk: Lohvinaŭ, 2015), pp. 26–31.
7. Terrorism itself does not play a major role in young prose, but it features in two works by Siarhiej Kalienda: 'Ehacentryst' (The egoist), Kalienda, 92–93, 97–98 and 'Paranoja' (Paranoia),126–29, 139.
8. Kryścina Kurčankova, 'Što-koĺviečy pra haradskich eĺfaŭ'. *Žvpzk*, pp. 144–52 (hereafter Kurčankova).
9. Aleś Jemialianaŭ, 'Teliepaetyka: Rytaryčnyja adkazy', *Dziejasloŭ*, 71 (2014), 60–64 (hereafter Jemialianaŭ).
10. This has nothing to do with the often used (and parodied) description of Belarus as a 'stable' country. For examples of parody see 'Čaroŭnaja krejdačka' in Ivaščanka, 61–74 (p. 64) where amidst violent repression the country is referred to as 'superstable'.
11. Carnegie was famous for self-help books, probably the most famous of which was *How to Win Friends and Influence People*, New York: Simon and Schuster, 1936.
12. The last two lines of this improbable dialogue are in English.
13. Aliona Bielanožka, 'Maladzik pa niebie chodzić', *Mdp* (hereafter Bielanožka), pp. 54–59.
14. Anatoĺ Ivaščanka, 'na sieansie ekzarcymu', *Vieršnick* (Miensk: Biellitfond, 2006), p. 36.
15. Etgar Keret (b. 1967) is an Israeli writer.
16. Jaŭhien Martynovič, 'Mora', *Mdp*, pp. 201–03 (hereafter Martynovič).

CHAPTER 4

Leadership, the Country and Squalor

SHAKESPEARE, 'Uneasy lies the head that wears a crown'
King Henry IV, Part II, III, i, 31

SHAKESPEARE, 'Then everything includes itself in power
Power into will, will into appetite;
And appetite a universal wolf'
Troilus and Cressida, I, iii, 119–20

In an authoritarian regime like Belarus, attention to the leadership is not only natural in scholarly and other non-fiction works written outside the country,[1] but also in some of the poetry and prose produced in Belarusian creative writing, insofar as relative freedom of expression still exists.[2] It is not unreasonable to regard the authorities' tolerance of critical writing as a kind of valve releasing pressure on the government; it may also be simply tolerance because of the very small editions of most fictional literature in Belarus. A relatively mild example is Anatoĺ Ivaščanka's 'Čaroŭnaja krejdačka' (The magic piece of chalk), in which he refers to the person behind the ruthless repression of demonstrations as '*haŭnakamandujučy*' (shit commander) (Ivaščanka, 64). In another story 'Save' Sieva goes from a violent computer game to thoughts of facing the AMON[3] at a street demonstration, but is in two minds, and only at the end joins the remains of it (Ivaščanka, 31–36). In his imaginative, quasi-documentary narratives the author makes clear the brutal savagery witnessed, particularly at the mass demonstrations in 2006 and 2010. Liolik Uškin (pen name of Alieś Novikaŭ, b. 1972) in his book *Jak adradzić VKL (Fielietony, humareski)* (How to regenerate the Grand Duchy of Lithuania [Feuilletons, humoresques]), offers mostly quasi-journalistic and humorous reactions to various political and other events, mainly from the middle of the first decade of the 21st century, although some pieces, including the last of them are purely imaginary. The book ends with 'Kalaradyč (hrafičny-fantastyčny trylier)' (Kalaradyč [a graphic-fantastic thriller]), but this cartoon will not be considered here. A review of a few of the purely verbal elements in the book, however, will give an impression of this writer's attitude and approach to leadership. Firstly, it should noted that Uškin's feuilletons and humoresques are set in a variety of places in Belarus, as he sketches comic aspects of post-Soviet reality. In 'Poŭny zaval' (A complete failure), for instance, the setting is Škloŭ where the President has just descended, in an attempt to stimulate growth and dissipate apathy. The phrase 'новы этап дзяржаўнага будаўніцтва' (a new stage in the building of the state) rings in people's ears. The difference between the older generation and the younger one is clearly reflected in an oral exam at the university following the presidential visit, as is seen in the following exchange between the examiner and a student:

> Выкладчык: 'Ну, што там у вас'?
> Студэнт: 'Білет нумар 13. Пералічыць асартымент тавараў, якія, як кантстатаваў прэзідэнт, цяжка знайсці на паліцах шклоўскай спажыўкааперацыі'.
> Выкладчык: 'Ну?!'
> Студэнт, чухаючы патыліцу: 'Можа, ноўтбукі?'
> Выкладчык: 'Як можна такога не ведаць! Мука, крупы, мясныя і рыбныя прадукты, ніткі, лямпачкі, мыйныя сродкі. Ну віншую — пойдзеце ў войска.'[4]

> (Teacher: 'Well, what have you got there?' Student: 'Ticket no. 13. Enumerate the goods which, as the president established, are hard to find on the shelves of Škloŭ stores'; Teacher: 'Well?!' Student, scratching the back of his head: 'Maybe notebooks?' Teacher: 'How can you not know such a thing! Flour, groats, meat and fish products, thread, light bulbs, washing materials. Well, I congratulate you — you will be going into the army.')

Other satire, some of it rather obvious, is nonetheless also amusing. For instance, in 'Jak myć dajarku' (How to wash a milkmaid), following an instruction from on high that milkmaids should be clean before going to bed, the director of a collective farm delivers a speech about how pig farmers and milkmaids (two significant professions in this context, as all but the youngest Belarusians know) should be cleaned. 'Jak halasavać pry talkovaj demakratyi' (How to vote in a sensible [stable] democracy) is also strongly satirical. More entertaining, however, is 'JeŭraBRSM' (EuroBelarusian Youth Organization) which contains some amusing exchanges with a young girl who has no clue who the Leader is, thinking perhaps that he might be a foreign pop singer or composer (Uškin, 51). Finally, from a book that is almost entirely satirical, may be mentioned 'Na apošnim dychańni' (With the last breath) in which Uškin describes the shock experienced by a convinced supporter of the regime working in the media, Jury Azaronak, who struggles when the leader, in the interests of economy, orders that all Belarusian television channels must follow the lead of independent film makers, as a result of which this loyal supporter finds himself sacked (Uškin, 24–25).

An even worse fate than Azaronak's is experienced by the eponymous heroine of Sieviaryn Kviatkoŭski's story 'Siabroŭka Prezydenta' (The President's girlfriend), a controller on the Miensk transport system who, having caught a fare-dodger and been told ironically that she is working on the personal instructions of the President, takes the words seriously. He has often addressed her personally on the television, filling her heart with happiness, and his words make her forget all the bad things in her life.[5] Acquiring the nickname of the title (Kviatkoŭski, 66), she begins to accept requests from naive members of the public to bring various matters to the attention of her 'boyfriend'. When she moves away from the station where she had previously lived and worked, she has to pay her own fare to get there; meanwhile her hero has issued a warning about fare-dodgers. One day, travelling to work on a trolleybus, she does not pay correctly, dreaming of her responsibilities and the manly features of her friend. Suddenly the vehicle stops and amidst the chaos He enters the trolleybus, making a presidential check, demanding that everybody show their ticket. When he reaches the controller and she cannot produce one, she is taken off the bus and shot (Kviatkoŭski, 69).

For a final example of direct satire on the leadership, Paval Kaściukievič's story 'Suka-krot' (The mole bitch) depicts a solemn ceremony at the Kurhan Slavy (Victory Mound) which is reduced to chaos by a mole. The following quotation will illustrate the eponymous animal's antics:

> 'Нават дыктатар не можа нічога парабіць з кратом. Гэтая сука (у сэнсе, крот) — проста чарнявая шэльма! [...] А здзеклівая жывёліна прыпускае далей — адпальвае па-мастацку: піруэты, па, нават патройныя сальты. Занураецца, выныpвае, таньчыць брэйк-дэнс, спалучаючы сінхроннае плаванне з фігурным коўзаннем. Сука-крот!' (Kaściukievič, 114–15)
>
> (Even a dictator can do nothing with a mole. This bitch (in the sense of a mole) was simply a dark little scoundrel! [...] And the mocking little animal carries on further — in masterly manner it carries out: pirouettes, pas, even triple somersaults. It buries down, digs its way up, performs break-dances, combining synchronic swimming with figure skating. This mole bitch!)

The Leader's cheeks twitch, shooting off the top of his epaulettes (Kaściukievič, 119). The great and the good who are assembled on the Mount produce many fantastic suppositions about what is going on. The Head of the Security Services eventually calls a candle-lit prayer meeting, after which everybody falls into a black hole that has been dug (Kaściukievič 120–21).

Finally may be mentioned a somewhat bizarre piece by the writer and political activist Taćciana Śnitko (pen-name of Jania Ždanovič), 'Kurs maladoha bajca: Mistyčnaje apaviadańnie'[6] (The course of a young warrior: A mystical story) which describes a young couple preparing for a demonstration (the metro has been closed), but they go home, depressed at its futility. The main themes are political dissidence, the ruthlessness of the KDB and police, with the addition of a rebellious but alcoholic journalist. Why the story is described as mystical is not entirely clear.

The direct and indirect disrespectful images of the Belarusian leadership illustrated in this section, both humorous and serious, are diverse in form and content, and often very inventive in their approaches to a familiar figure.

Miensk, the Provinces and Abroad; Idealization and Squalor

SHAKESPEARE, 'Alas, poor country', *Macbeth*, V, iii, 164–65

Miensk

Many people, including writers, have commented with anything from amusement to indignation on the number of (far from unpleasant) streets and squares in central Miensk that are named after people and phenomena emblematic of the Soviet era (Marx,[7] Engels, Lenin, International, Communist and so on). Young poets have reacted against the impersonality of the city, and there are also several pictures in young prose of, for example, appallingly squalid and dangerous entrance halls in Miensk and other locations. It is against this background that Aleś Jemialianaŭ's very personal essay, 'Vieršatop'[8] should be seen. In it he reflects on Miensk streets and poetic experience, beginning: 'Люблю менскія вуліцы. Але ж не ўсе, а толькі з цікавымі паэтычнымі назвамі' (Jemialianaŭ, 61) (I love the streets of Miensk, but not all of them, only those with interesting poetic names). He illustrates various streets with poetic names or personal associations, such as 'Soniečnaja' (Sunny), 'Viasiolkavaja' (Rainbow) and 'Pryhožaja' (Beautiful), for instance, ending by expressing apprehension that they will disappear under skyscrapers and other developments. In many cases only the name of poetic-sounding streets will be left: 'Як чалавек, ад якога засталося толькі імя, а ўсё астатнае страчана — ані хаты, ані роду, ані племені.' (Jemialianaŭ, 62) (Like a person who has a name but everything else is lost — home, race and tribe.) In an untitled piece by Vaĺžyna Mort, 'Čas zbiehaje adsiuĺ by uciakač...' (Time runs away from here like a fugitive), she describes walking backwards and forwards criss-crossing the town only to find that she cannot recall any building, any tree, monument or person (Mort, 77–79). Mort's best known early prose piece, 'Hopniki' (Rowdies) describes vividly life in a big city during a heat wave, in a characteristically frank manner. It begins with the narrator vainly attempting to make a phone call, going on to masturbation (and consequent shame before her waiting lunch and the furniture) to a number of protests against what she sees as a shitty world; the reproduction of sounds from outside is impressively dyspeptic including the thought as she hears cries of 'Happy Birthday!' that the best way to put out the candles on the cake is to piss on them (Mort, 98–104). The story's closing passage is far from the least bleak, belonging at least to the section on squalor in this book as the descriptions of Miensk:

Я прачынаюся ад нясьцерпнай сьпякоты. Ізноў лета. Ізноў раніца. Ізноў гопнікі пад акном. Скура прыліпла да цела, як мокрая адзежа. Не люблю. Тэмпэратура большая за месячны заробак. У маіх трусах корпаецца жывая жоўтая малпа, і я не магу нават зьвесці ног. (Mort, 104)

(I wake up from the unbearable heat. Again summer. Again morning. Again there are young rowdies beneath my window. My skin has stuck to my body like damp clothing. I do not like it. The temperature is higher than my monthly wage. A live yellow monkey is digging around in my knickers, and I cannot even close my legs.)

Maryja Roŭda takes a particularly dim view in 'Kliničny vypadak', when she reflects on the city: 'Што Менск — там нават ружы прадаюць, як шлюх: у чырвоным падманным святле.' (Roŭda, 156) (As for Miensk, there even roses are sold like whores: in a red, deceptive light.) There are more roses in the subtitle of another story by Roŭda: 'Hetkaj biady. Aĺbo Kachańnie, jak štambavanaja ruža' (What a misfortune. Or Love like a rosebush) (Roŭda, 265). Other even less favourable images of Miensk will be mentioned later.

The Provinces and Urban Settlements

Uladź Harbacki in his *Pieśni traliejbusnych rahuliaŭ* (discussed in the first chapter) both praises and laments his native Viciebsk, and Aleś Byčkoŭski in his *Horad za 101-m kilamietram* describes vividly a hellish industrial settlement.

Probably the most bleak and memorable of all is the short but powerful debut novel by Źmicier Hud who was born in Homiel in 1986, *Poŭdzień-3* (South-3).[9] The narration begins in a leisurely manner, with much detail, depicting an industrial suburb full of big smog-covered furnaces and with identical buildings: 'тыпавыя дамы нагадвалі пашыхтаваных на пляцы жаўнераў, апранутых у аднолькавую вайсковую ўніформу' (Hud, 7) (standard buildings resembled soldiers lined up on the parade ground dressed in identical military uniforms). The anti-social young inhabitants of this god-forsaken place often meet outside a store, waiting for it to open and re-supply them with alcohol. The central character of the novel stands apart: with the cruel nickname of Hlist, he was isolated and bullied at school and, after a teenage prank that goes wrong, is now regarded as a traitor and a coward. He is a pitiful character as is shown in this early description of him:

Гліст, напэўна, быў нават крыху падобны да толькі што выгнанага з раю біблейскага Адама: гэткі ж бездапаможны і безабаронны, сам-насам з варожым навакольным светам і сваім смяротным целам, якое Гліст ледзь узняў з ложку, бо яно было зьнясіленае посталкагольнай млосцю. (Hud, 31)

(Hlist was probably a little like the biblical Adam just after being expelled from Paradise, similarly helpless and defenceless, totally alone in the hostile world around him and with his mortal body, which Hlist could hardly raise from his bed, as it was weakened by post-alcoholic sickness.)

Only one of the locals, no less of a drinker than the bullies, nicknamed Praviednik (The righteous one) or Jesus on account of his long hair, makes an attempt to befriend him, which, however, ends badly. Hud paints the background of many of the young people, almost all damaged by alcohol at home, including a girl, Esmieraĺda, who also shows sympathy for Hlist to the point of taking him with her to bed, but all ends in fiasco (Hud, 49). Far the worst person in this settlement's collection of dysfunctional characters is a ruthless money-lender and gangster, Kavun, who in the end proves the cause of Hlist's torture and death. Later, on an unusually sunny day, the victim receives a funeral far better than anything he had known when alive (Hud, 96–97). At the end the drunks realize that Hlist was their friend, now a dead friend. *Poŭdzień-3* is far more absorbing in its plot and detail than the above summary can imply. It is one of the most memorable and grimly convincing pictures of provincial alcohol-soaked low life that the present writer has encountered for a long time.

Maryja Maliaŭka's already mentioned story. 'Žyvaja ryba' contains a less violent but none the less bleak picture of a little town in southern Belarus that has partly been built over a Jewish cemetery:

> Канец 90-х. Невялікі гарадок на поўдні Беларусі здаваўся змрочным, як быццам там заўсёды быў прадвячэрні час — гадзінаў чатыры-пяць вечара ў асеннюю пару. Хоць, вядома, было і лета, шмат сонца. Але запомніўся гэты самы няпэўны час сутак, калі здаецца, што ўсё святло выпілі, а дабратворная цемра яшчэ не прыхавала голае няўтульнае наваколле. (Maliaŭka, 190)

> (The end of the 90s. The little town in southern Belarus seemed gloomy as if it were always the time before evening — about four to five in the autumn. Although, of course, it was summer, and there was plenty of sun. But one recalls that same uncertain twilight hour when it seemed that all the light of the world had been drunk up, and the benevolent darkness had not yet covered up the bare, comfortless surroundings.)

Village life has been mentioned in several places earlier in the book and therefore does not require separate treatment here.

Travel and Life Abroad

Viĺnia is a city to which Belarusians feel particularly close. A humorous account of women from Ašmiany smuggling food, cosmetics and other goods is given in Kaściukievič's 'Ajčyna kantrabanda' (The contraband fatherland). The 'aunties' buy Belarusian goods and sell them in Viĺnia, buying there more sophisticated items to bring home. They describe the (now) Lithuanian city as a wonderland and they adapt the title of Karatkievič's celebrated novel, by saying 'Chrystos pryziamliŭsia ŭ Viĺni' (Chrystos came to earth in Viĺnia)

(Kaściukievič, 6).[10] The language used in this entertaining story appears to be authentic to Ašmiany.

Sieviaryn Kviatkoŭski offers an impressionistic picture of this city in 'Viĺnia ŭ kancy tuneliu' (Viĺnia at the end of a tunnel). The contrast between the quality of life in early morning Miensk and Viĺnia is very plain to the narrator (Kviatkoŭski, 17–18), who, despite his admiration, sees the Lithuanians as ghosts and not only ghosts of the many cultural figures of the past (Kviatkoŭski, 13). In a bar he meets a Belarusian called Marek who drives him to a place near the border, where at dinner everybody except one old man speaks Belarusian. There is a lively conversation in which the narrator explains humorously various aspects of his native country, but when the old man asks him about the Belarusian leader and gets a very negative reply, the visitor is thrown out and set down on the road to Miensk (Kviatkoŭski, 19–20). A few days later an unknown Lithuanian rings to say that they had shown on television some crazy Belarusian who had asked to be put up in a police cell (Kviatkoŭski, 20–21).

Maryja Roŭda in 'Kliničny vypadak' describes how her narrator visits Germany, and when her gnome has, for some reason, gone back to Miensk, she travels to the North Sea 'на п'яным нахабным ветры' (in its drunken insolent wind) and stares out 'перад санлівымі абрысамі Даніі' (towards the sleepy outlines of Denmark) (Roŭda, 157).

Arciom Kavalieŭski is more abstract but no less vivid in his story 'Vandroŭnik' (The traveller), which opens with some typically bold images:

> Вандроўкі, бы эскалатары. Яны лагодзяць здранцвеласць пачуццяў, аднаўляюць іх, вывозячы на паверхню новае прасторы. Ты ўсміхаешся кожнаму новаму месцу, а потым захлёбваешся кіслымі ванітамі салодкіх уражанняў [...] Цывілізацыі няма. [...] Цывілізацыя бы зубная паста: усё адно выплёўваецца... (Kavalieŭski, 122)
>
> (Travels are like escalators. They gratify our rusty feelings, bring them out on to the surface of new spaciousness. You smile at each new place, and then you choke on the bitter vomit of sweet impressions [...] There is no civilization [...] Civilization is like toothpaste; you are going to spit it out anyway...)

As with the themes of village life or squalor and hooliganism, there are many more tales of journeys and travel elsewhere in this book.

Squalor, Violence and Alcohol

In Shakespeare there is a considerable number of references to drinking, like Parolles's comment to an acquaintance: 'Drunkenness is his best virtue' (Shakespeare, *All's Well That Ends Well*, IV, iii, 249–50), but few could be less appropriate to Siarhiej Kalienda (b. 1985), whose 'Vomiting' is discussed later in this section.

Hud's powerful debut novel mentioned above falls into all these categories. Uladź Harbacki's detailed description of being attacked by a gang near his flat (Harbacki, 74–75) is likewise as relevant here as it was in the first chapter. Apart from her sexuality, which she clearly relishes, Nasta Mancevič paints a bleak picture of her surroundings, whether it is in 'Pazl' (A puzzle) also discussed in the first chapter, or in her re-creation of the traditional story of the three bears, 'Kazka' (A fairy story) where Mašeńka should have come in various sizes for the three bears, but as it is explained to the youngest bear:

> Разумееш, сынку, тут у нашым лесе, у гэтым засраным зарасніку жыве толькі адна Машэнька. Таму даводзіцца дзяліцца з усімі... (Mancevič, 17)
>
> (Understand, my dear son, in our forest, in these shitty bushes, there lives only one Mašeńka. For that reason she will have to be shared between us all...)

The last short paragraph is equally dismissive:

> Вось такая вось, рабяткі, гісторыя. І ўсё-тка я ў ёй разумею... Але ж мы, блядзь, не ў лесе! (Mancevič, 17)
>
> (That, guys, that's what the story was like. And all the same I understand in it... But we, after all, fuck it, are not in a forest!)

Two stories by Alaksiej Palačanski are worth mentioning here. In 'Pad stoĺliu' (Under the ceiling) he depicts a box-like airless flat in which the narrator feels trapped, with the ceiling seeming to get lower and lower, rather in the manner of Edgar Allan Poe. Physical squalor here is matched by the terrible events of the narrator's life, such as his sister's stabbing of their mother. A kind of release comes with an all-destroying fire, contrasted with brilliant snow outside, although his family have all fled. In the already mentioned story 'Jak zakopvali duby' there is a vivid description of an 'official committee' coming to a homestead on a mission of destruction, while the mother and her boy hide in a barn and watch through a crack in the wood:

> Мужчыны гаварылі і рухаліся вельмі хутка без бачных на тое прычын, яны ўсё рабілі рэзка — нечакана, як у старых нямых фільмах. (Palačanski, 101)
>
> (The men spoke and moved very quickly for no visible reason, they did everything harshly and unexpectedly, like in old silent films.)

They bring machines to destroy the oaks, and depart leaving a wasteland:

> Усе яны ўтваралі суцэльны гул, ператваралі чыстае спелае поле ў смярдзючы іржавы цэх, з далёкім рэхам лязгату і матарызны. (Palačanski, 103)
>
> (They were all creating a wall of noise, transforming a pure ripe field into a stinking rusty workshop, with the distant echo of clanking and motors.)

* * * * *

Alcohol is a frequent theme in the work of young (and not only young) Belarusian writers. Before turning to it and the often concomitant vomiting, it may be worth mentioning one story about the authorities' attempts to rid the country of this scourge: Siarhiej Kalienda's 'Niavykrutka' (No way out) describes the banning of alcohol in the 1980s leading to an urban settlement's apparent improvement, although in reality it produced a huge increase in violence, suicides and drug taking. As the author notes at the end: 'Галоўнае, што ніхто не п'е. Магілы маладзеюць, могілкі растуць...' (Kalienda, 174) (The main thing is that nobody is drinking. The graves are getting younger. The cemeteries are growing...)

A grimly realistic glimpse of alcohol and its consequences is given by Paviel Kapanski (b. 1986) in his story 'Žyćcio z vialikaj litary Ž'[11] (Life with a capital L), in which a young man, returning home after a domestic argument, comes across a hopelessly drunk man. The essence of the story is the battle with his conscience: whether to carry this filthy alcoholic on his shoulder or to abandon him. The voice of his wife looking for him and (most improbably) saying that all is forgiven apparently enables the young man to abandon the drunk with a clear conscience. The moral of the story, if it has one, is unclear. Drunkenness is also near the centre of Sieviaryn Kviatkoŭski's satire on journalistic and literary life in 'Šampanskaje ŭ šafie' (The champagne is in the cupboard) (Kviatkoŭski, 51–62).

Maksim, the main character in Andrej Adamovič's *Taŭścila i lieŝč*, apparently revived his hard-won bream by being sick on it. Vomiting figures widely in Siarhiej Kalienda's world. 'Vanity' (Vomiting) is a prime example of his dyspeptic views, tracing the life of a photographer Danila Lakanaŭ from childhood at eleven, when he is sick at table, after being forced to eat revolting food and whipped by his father, to when he was sixteen and has come to believe that vomiting is a way to purify his soul. It is also a point of 'romantic' contact with an anorexic girl, as they are sick together. A curious feature of the story is that numeration of the sections goes from 0.6 to -0.1.[12] Lakanaŭ's interests are philosophical (as might be expected from his name) as well as crudely physical. The following excerpt from section 0.5 gives a vivid example of his acute feeling of alienation:

> Данілу Лаканаву толькі шаснаццаць, ён падлетак, але яму ўжо абрыдла жыць у гэтым наваколлі. Сярод людзей, жывёл, раслін, вычварэнцаў, дэгенератаў, філосафаў, мастакоў, сярод аўтамабіляў, тэхнікі, вялізарных будынкаў. ЁН НЕ ХОЧА БЫЦЬ ДЗІЦЁМ АСФАЛЬТУ, ЁН НЕ ХОЧА БЫЦЬ ДЗІЦЁМ ТЭХНАКРАТЫІ, ЁН НЕ ХОЧА БЫЦЬ ДЗІЦЁМ АТРУЧАНЫХ ЛЮДЗЕЙ, ЁН НЕ ХОЧА БЫЦЬ ІХ ПАКАЛЕННЕМ! (Kalienda, p. 13)

(Danila Lakanaŭ is only sixteen, he is a youth, but he is already revolted by living in these surroundings. Among people, animals, vegetation, freaks, degenerates, philosophers and artists, among cars, technology, immense buildings. HE DOES NOT WANT TO BE A CHILD OF ASPHALT, HE DOES NOT WANT TO BE A CHILD OF TECHNOCRACY, HE DOES NOT WANT TO BE A CHILD OF POISONED PEOPLE, HE DOES NOT WANT TO BE THEIR GENERATION!)

In a later section (0.3) he describes vomiting as ecstasy, inner cleansing, emptiness and lightness in the world:

І ён цяпер знайшоў адзіны шлях, дзе няма хлусні, дзе ты адкрыты ў першую чаргу сам з сабою — ванітаваць, такім ён бачыў шлях. (Kalienda, 17)

(and he had found the only path where there was no lying, where you are open in the first place only to yourself — vomiting, that was where he saw his path.)

* * * * *

To create a chapter linking leadership with frequently bleak views of the Leader's country and with vomiting, should not be viewed as a logical, Freudian or any other connection, but merely as a matter of authorial convenience.

Notes to Chapter 4

1. Apart from two books published anonymously in Miensk, Warsaw and Moscow, entitled *Idyjot samy nastajaščy* (2000, 2001), two major academic studies in English throwing light on the leadership are: Andrew Wilson, *Belarus: The Last European Dictatorship* (New Haven and London: Yale University Press, 2011), and Brian Bennett, *The Last Dictatorship in Europe: Belarus under Lukashenko* (London: Hurst and Co, 2011). A far more entertaining work, throwing light on the leadership through folklore and humour is: Anastasiya Astapova, *Negotiating Belarusianness: Political Folklore Betwixt and Between* (Tartu: University of Tartu Press), 2015.
2. Freedom of expression is a relative concept. During preparation for my book on young Belarusian poets (*Spring Shoots*) I found several collections of verse, openly or by implication, critical of the leadership, but when the translation was due to be published in Belarusian (*Ruń*) the publisher in Miensk asked that three lines cited from two poets (neither of whose books had proved difficult for me to obtain) be removed, suggesting that otherwise 'we will all be arrested'. Only one of the two poets could be contacted, but he accepted this change without protest.
3. Mobile detachment of militia for special purposes.
4. Liolik Uškin, *Jak adradzič VKL (fielietony, humareski)* (Minsk: Biblijatečka Centraĺnaja, 2016) (hereafter Uškin), p. 17.
5. Another example of falling in love with a figure on television is Taćciana Barysik's 'Teliehistoryja' (A television story) in which a disabled woman falls in love with a

female presenter, but fails in her attempts to express her feelings for this remote object of her adoration (Barysik, 60–63).

6. Taćciana Śnitko, 'Kurs maladoha bajca: Mistyčnaje apaviadańnie', *Źvzpk*, pp. 224–36.
7. Karl Marx Street is just one of those in the capital that were built, very thoroughly, by German prisoners.
8. This word, an amalgam of the Belarusian words for poem and place does not appear to exist elsewhere, rather like the title of Jemialianaŭ's collection of poems, *Parasoniečnaść* (Minsk: Knihazbor, 2013).
9. Źmicier Hud, *Poŭdzień-3* (Minsk: Halijafy, 2013) (hereafter Hud).
10. Uladzimir Karatkievič, *Chrystos pryziamliŭsia ŭ Harodni: Jevanhieĺlie ad Iudy* (Minsk: Mastackaja litaratura, 1966).
11. Paviel Kapanski, 'Žyćcio z vialikaj litary Ž', *Hienijuš loci*, pp. 107–09.
12. Doubtless it is pure coincidence that Voĺha Hapiejeva (who wrote a sensitive introduction to Kalienda's debut novel) has eccentric numeration in her play 'Rekanstrukcyja nieba' (Reconstruction of the sky): Voĺha Hapiejeva, *Rekanstrukcyja nieba* (Minsk, Lohvinaŭ, 2003), pp. 91–139.

CHAPTER 5

Writing about Language and the Nature of Its Use

SHAKESPEARE, 'O let my books be then the eloquence
And dumb presages of my speaking
Sonnets, 23, 9–10

Language as a subject

Language is, of course, a central element in writing, and young Belarusian prose writers are as aware of this as the poets, although there are far less impassioned declarations of love for the national language in prose than there were in poetry from the 1960s and earlier, up to the present day.[1] Specific and dialectal language has been noted earlier in relation to the unconventional and sometimes difficult youth slang used in Anatoĺ Ivaščanka's quasi-reminiscences in *Anatalohija*, the title of which is an invented word comparable to Aleś Jemialianaŭ's *Teliepaetyka*. Swearing and other non-normative forms of language will be considered later. There is plenty of 'bad language', incidentally, in Kiryla Duboŭski's 'Bielaruskaja mova' (The Belarusian language) in which the narrator tells his friend about a terrible dream he has just experienced of a muzhik in full peasant costume, who announces 'Я Беларуская Мова! Няхай не будзе ў цябе іншых моваў, апроч мяне!'[2] (I am the Belarusian Language! May you have no other languages apart from me!). In Kryścina Kurčankova's already mentioned 'Što-koĺviečy pra haradskich eĺfaŭ' the Goblin's parents cannot forgive him for not accepting his fatherland, where people speak in 'their' language (i.e. Belarusian). The Goblin, however, does not want to be a 'nationalist', favouring a punk world of universal love and beer (*Žvzpk*, 148–49). Maryja Roŭda in 'Kliničny vypadak' brings some humour to her description of the struggle of the German 'gnome' with the complexities of the Belarusian language (Roŭda, 161). There is more pathos in 'Daroha damoŭ' (The way home) by Mikita Volkaŭ[3] in which Nadzieja, the daughter of teachers, seems to be in love with Janak, who is from the simplest of families, partly because she romantically regards him as being at the heart of the people, having heard him use a rare Belarusian expression (Volkaŭ, 71). She then sets about creating from him the ideal she craves through language, culture and religion. This ill-judged attempt to create another person in a desired image ends in predictable misunderstandings and tragedy as on the way home he meets wild pigs, but instead of escaping walks straight towards them and his death (Volkaŭ, 73).

The comprehensibility of the Belarusian language is touched on in Alisa Biziajeva's 'Tramvajny son' where the narrator in a bookshop takes up books in turn:

> кнігі на мове, якую больш нідзе не разумеюць. Сёння ў сініх пераплётах. Трапляе на цудоўнае, нібыта ёй самой напісанае: 'Белыя фіранкі нясмела цягнуліся з вокнаў да кветніка. Быццам хочача нарваць сябе трохі цюльпанаў на малюнак'. (Biziajeva, 179)
>
> (books in a language which people no longer understand anywhere. Now in blue covers. She comes across something wonderful that seems to have been written by herself: 'The white curtains timidly stretched from the windows towards the flower bed. As if wishing to pick for themselves a few tulips to make a pattern.')

If the books in Biziajeva's story are in a language that nobody understands, the contraband smugglers in Paval Kaściukievič's 'Ajčyna kantrabanda' speak in a very particular way using words that have survived centuries of attempts to drive them out:

> мова ашмянскіх цётак точыцца словамі старажытных друідаў, якія на злосць шматвекавым захопнікам выжылі... (Kaściukievič, 6)
>
> (the language of the Ašmiany aunties is sprinkled with words of the ancient Druids, which have survived for centuries to the fury of foreign invaders...)

The perhaps hardly less ancient (but certainly more enduring) use of swear words will be considered later. Firstly may be mentioned an interesting story by Źmicier Bajarovič, 'Kvatera na Pieramozie' (A flat on Victory Square), a longish piece (in Belarusian) with interjected lines in Russian (like a chorus, but together reading as a poem). This could be seen as an example of a *creative* use of the generally negative bilingualism enshrined in the 1995 referendum. The story is of a woman whose life has been ruined by speculators and unwanted pregnancy, and particularly by the loss of the man she truly loves. But when she reads his Russian-language jingle interspersed between the lines of the Belarusian text, she howls with grief. Here is the verse reconstructed from the insertions, for what it is worth:

> мы с тобой, как две руки
> мы друг друга моем
> я тебе пишу стихи
> ты их пьёшь запоем
> то ломаем на куски
> то опять построим

мы с тобою дураки
и друг друга стоим. (Bajarovič, 75–77)

(You and I are like two hands / we wash each other / I write verses to you / You gulp them down / now we break everything to pieces / now we build them up again / you and I are fools / and are worthy of each other.)

The story ends with an unambiguous statement:

У кватэры на Перамозе ты прайгравала свайго каханага
А потым чытала паміж радкоў яго верш,
І галасіла.

(In the flat on Victory Square you lost your beloved / And then read his verse between the lines / And howled.)

Writing as a subject

Although science fiction and the process of writing are not naturally associated, there are two comments on writing in Aleś Byčkoŭski's 'Ciahnik liosaŭ (remix)' (The train of fates [remix]). The first states a general political problem, and the second is drawn from personal experience:

Нам не даюць пісаць праўду, і не плоцяць, каб маўчалі. (Byčkoŭski, 57)

(They do not let us write truth and do not pay us to be silent.)

Ёсць такая хвароба — пісьменніцкі сверб. Гэта калі спачатку пішаш, а потым ужо чытаеш напісанае і зусім нічога не разумееш. (Byčkoŭski, 59)

(There is such an illness — the itch to write. That is when you first write and then when you read it you understand absolutely nothing.)

Sieviaryn Kviatkoŭski in 'Sinjaje vakno' (The blue window) describes his own drive to write (almost from childhood) regardless of quality, although he is no graphomaniac. He paints a picture of the sweetness and torture of writing (Kviatkoŭski, 91).

The (anti-) hero from Siarhiej Kalienda's 'Paranoja' (Paranoia), Frank, is a public-relations man who writes mainly about male dominance over women. His particular obsession is with real-life violent tragedies that his writing seems (to him) to have anticipated, especially terrorism (Kalienda, 129–30). One of his girlfriends, however, shocks Frank by showing that life is 'worse' than the violent porn he writes (Kalienda, 135). Near the end of the story he is offered a new subject by a pleasant man, but it turns out to be exactly what he had been writing:

... як толькі яго апавядальнік пачаў сваю гісторыю, Франк адчуў, што яго зараз проста ванітуе, не ад спіртнога, а ад самой гісторыі, якую ён

> чуў. Гэтая гісторыя жыцця супадала з ягонай гісторыяй на паперы, з ягонай гісторыяй, якая ляжала зараз у рэдактара... (Kalienda, 147)

> (... as soon as his narrator began his story, Frank felt that he was immediately going to be sick, not from the spirits he had drunk, but from the very story he had heard. This story from life corresponded to his story on paper, to his story that was at that moment lying with the editor...)

Finally from earlier in the story here is a description of Frank's painful early-morning awakening to writing:

> З галавы Франка выява за выявай нараджалася новая аповесць, за акном ужо прагледжваў світанак. Хутка на працу, а ён як заведзены ўсё пісаў і пісаў. (Kalienda. 128)

> (From Frank's head, event by event, was being born a new story, beyond the window dawn was already peeping. Soon it would be work, but he, as if wound up by clockwork, was still writing and writing.)

Finally may be mentioned one of two pieces by Anka Upala that consist entirely of words beginning with 'p', 'Padrobny paet' (A detailed poet), in which the eponymous young poet visits a pillar of the literary establishment, Piatro Piatrovič Pichto-Publicki, ending by the latter inwardly rebuking his visitor:

> Постмадэрністы паскудныя — падумаў Пятро Пятровіч, пачухваючы пад пахамі. — Паказаў паднаготную. Панапрыязджаюць, панапрыкідаюцца паэтамі... Падробкі! Пайду паэму напішу... (Upala 63)

> ('Filthy postmodernists', thought Piatro Piatrovič, scratching his crotch. I have shown him all there is to know. They come in droves, pretending to be poets... Fakes! I'll go and write a narrative poem...)

Incidentally, the other poem consisting of words beginning only with 'p', 'Panadzielak pačynajecca paślia piatnicy' (Monday begins after Friday) may well exemplify Piatro Piatrovič's 'filth' starting as it does in one direction but at the end starting again in a different one (Upala, 58–61).

The Nature of Young Prose Writing

To begin with the excellent writing by Natalka Charytaniuk (who, incidentally, wrote a thesis on the work of one of the best English stylists, Julian Barnes), it must be said that much has already been mentioned in the treatment of other works discussed earlier, so that omission of many writers here is far from meaning that they are unworthy of attention, or that their stylistic achievements have been overlooked. Charytaniuk's very well written family history has been discussed extensively in Chapter 2, but is worth mentioning again as a particularly fine piece. But before leaving the topic of writers discussed elsewhere, it should be said that one of the best stylists of his generation, Paval Kaściukievič, has been considered in many other contexts, but not in this section.[4] Perhaps also worth mentioning is Marharyta Latyškievič, already referred to in Chapter 2, who has a very good command of narration, albeit with a slight tendency to wordiness. Also notable is Aliaksiej Palačanski who uses richly elaborate language. Several stories illustrating the skill of this very promising writer have been discussed elsewhere, especially, 'Jak zakopvali duby' and 'Na kavalki'.

Apart from Andrej Adamovič's rather difficult language, mentioned in Chapter 2, there are other aspects of writing worth discussing. Siarhiej Balachonaŭ in his novel and his stories is a master of historical language, as is, indeed, Anton Bryĺ (b. 1982).[5] Balachonaŭ allows into his language a number of crude (barely disguised) swear words, of which four examples will suffice: бл*дзтве (whoremongering), у*бка (fuck-up), х*я (prick), бл*дун (whoremonger) (Balachonaŭ, 155, 189, 208). Kiryl Stasieĺka in a story 'Dva dni' (Two days) uses as narrator a drug-taking book illustrator who longs for fame and money without working, railing against his alarm clock using in short order 'Fuck' and 'Blin' (Stasieĺka, 136). Freeness with foreign swear words and relative modesty with native ones[6] is not confined to Stasieĺka and his narrator in young Belarusian prose or poetry (see McMillin, Macaronic).

More interesting is the account by Uladź Harbacki of how he first became aware of the worth of the Belarusian language from the songs that his Old Believer grandmother sang him as a child, and from the way, coming from a village, she spoke:

> Але яшчэ больш разяваў я рот, калі пачынала бабуля размаўляць з намі. Яна размаўляла не па-расейску, як гэта было зазвычай у горадзе, яна размаўляла, як мне тады здавалася, на мове, на якой размаўляюць казачныя героі. І я разумеў яе! (Harbacki, 6).
>
> (But I opened my mouth even more when my granny spoke with us. She spoke not in Russian as was the usual thing in the city, she spoke, as it seemed to me at the time, in a language spoken by fabulous heroes. And I understood it!)

* * * * *

Imagery and word play have been mentioned elsewhere, but two miniatures by Źmicier Bajarovič are worth mentioning as examples of the latter: 'Z novym chodam' (Happy New year / move) where a chess match during the holiday celebrations allows the author to have fun with the near homonyms, 'hod' (year) and 'chod' (move). In another miniature, 'biĺjard' (billiards) the arrival of his girlfriend reminds him of billiards, leading to play with another two words, 'abcas' (heel) and 'abzac' (paragraph): 'Абцас — абзац. Адзін, бо іншы стаў ахвярай хворай слізоты' (Bajarovič, 81) (Heel — paragraph. Only one, for the other one became a victim of sick slipperiness). Before leaving Bajarovič, two examples of his use of imagery could also be mentioned. In 'čarka' (the cup) he compares people leaving the third floor of a shop for the lunch break to water from an overturned cup gradually dripping off the edge of a table (Bajarovič, 44). The other illustration is closer to the theme of writing in this chapter, 'drennyja slovy' (bad words):

> дрэнныя словы
> Занядбаныя будоўлі, як недапісаныя вершы. І там і там з цягам часу з'яўляюцца дренныя словы,'
>
> (bad words // neglected building sites are like unfinished poems. In both places bad words appear.)

Another imaginative writer who introduces some bold imagery into his prose is Arciom Kavalieŭski, who opens the first story in his second book, the already mentioned 'Malako', with a striking sentence:

> У яго былі непаголеныя думкі пра вернасць, а на далонях спалі аднастайныя жаданні быць пачварнікам 101-й старонкі ў кнізе вяртанняў. (Kavalieŭski, 105)
>
> (He had unshaven thoughts about fidelity, and on his palms slept monotonous longings to be a little monster on the 101st page of a book of returns.)

Kavalieŭski's verse in his debut volume, *Admyslovyja hulni* (Special games, 2003) was clearly that of an avant-garde poet, devoted to assonance, repetition, and a variety of games.[7] In *Addalienaść i addanaść*, however, the ludic element is less to the fore, although assonance is still important and the verse very imaginative. In his prose he seems to enjoy almost childlike play with names, as in this example from 'Amaĺ usio' (Almost everything): 'Федзя — з'еў мядзведзя' (Kavalieŭski, 108) (Fiedzia ate a bear). In addition to this writer's use of imagery earlier in the book, it may be worth mentioning some further interesting images like that used by the narrator of 'Long Play' who worries that his life is too geometrically perfect:

> дзе менавіта варта спыніцца, каб раз і назаўсёды адчуць перамогу над уласнай бясстрашнасцю й геаметрычна дакладнай манерай паводзінаў? Дзе спыніцца й перавесці дыханне? Ягонае прыватнае жыццё было сапраўдным музеем, уваход у які па льготных квітках строга рэгламентаваўся. (Kavalieŭski, 117)
>
> (where precisely should he stop in order to feel once and for all victory over his own impassiveness and his precisely geometrical manner of behaving? Where should he stop and catch his breath? His private life was a true museum, entry to which with concessionary tickets was strictly regulated.)

This image is later extended at greater length by the author (Kavalieŭski, 117–18). Another extended image is found in the already mentioned 'Vandroŭnik' where amongst a general sense of alienation we find the somewhat startling: 'Жанчына — катрынка. Мужчына — кампосцер' (Woman is a barrel organ. Man is a ticket punch) (Kavalieŭski, 123), images that are also subsequently developed further. More concise is 'Raźnica' (The difference) where an insecure young female narrator tries to appear defenceless to please her man, whom she compares to a mouse trap waiting for the cheese to lure someone (her) in (Kavalieŭski, 119–20).

* * * * *

Like history in the last chapter of this book, language is an inalienable and vital part of Belarusian national consciousness. Moreover its use in imagery, whether ludic or not, plays an important part in the literature that helps to keep the language alive. The work of young writers, including their reflections about and use of Belarusian, plays a vital role in preserving the nation's identity, in the face not only of official indifference and hindrance, but also of the prosaic and materialistic Zeitgeist dominating not only in Belarus, but in many countries of the world.

Notes to Chapter 5

1. The fact that the Leader has stated that nothing of worth can be said in Belarusian is as notorious as it is incorrect.
2. Kiryla Duboŭski, 'Bielaruskaja mova', *Hienijuš loci*, p. 85.
3. Mikita Volkaŭ, 'Daroha damoŭ', *Mdp*, pp. 70–73 (hereafter Volkaŭ).
4. One of Kaściukievič's recent books, which epitomizes his command of style is: *Plan Babarozy: Siamiejnaja saha* (Minsk, Lohvinaŭ: 2016).
5. For more detail see Arnold McMillin, 'Pradstaŭnik redkaj dynastyi: Anton Frańcišak Bryĺ', *Polymia*, 11 (2016), 127–38 (hereafter McMillin, Bryĺ).
6. In fact, Belarusian swearing is very akin or even identical to Russian, so the word 'native' has limited validity. Maryja Martysievič's essay on Belarusian bad language remains one of the best and wittiest to be written: Maryja Martysievič, 'Pašli mianie pa-bielarusku', *Cmoki liatuć na vyrast* (Minsk: Lohvinaŭ, 2008), pp. 56–63.
7. See Arnold McMillin, *Writing in a Cold Climate: Belarusian Literature from the 1970s to the Present Day*, Publications of The Modern Humanities Research Association, 18 (London: Maney Publishing for the MHRA, 2010), pp. 1019–26

CHAPTER 6

History

SHAKESPEARE, 'There is a history in all men's lives,
Figuring the nature of the times deceas'd'
King Henry IV, Part II, III, i, 80–81

Uladzimir Karatkievič laid the foundation of Belarusian historical fantasy, although it would be difficult to see his direct influence on any of the writers in this chapter. Nonetheless he is a constant presence, for example, in Paval Kaściukievič's description of the visit of the Ašmiany smugglers to Vilnia who make a transparent reference to one of his best-known novels, mentioned in the previous chapter. Hardly less important is Uladzimir Arloŭ in setting an excellent model for potential young historical prose writers, outstanding amongst whom is Anton Frańcišak Bryl (b. 1982) a master of historical poetry and prose with a fine sense of language, control of plot and sense of humour, whose work abounds in superstitions and myths, and who, incidentally, disagrees fundamentally with Valiancin Akudovič's concept of myth (for detail see McMillin, Bryl).[1] What follows is a view of his remarkable novella *Jan Jalmužna*,[2] which like the poems shows the author's lively historical imagination as well as genuine learning, displayed with mastery of language and unostentatious humour life in Prince Haštaŭt's castle at Hieraniony in the west of Belarus, and the exploits of the eponymous hero Jan Jalmužna, a talented and ambitious kitchen boy. The novella's Prologue begins with a powerful scene in the castle after the death of former ruler Alexander, Grand Duke of Lithuania, depicting the disorienting effect this event had on the nobles as well as introducing some of the other characters. The nature of belief at that time is also shown at this early stage when a party of unknown horsemen appear to ride straight through a crowd, an event deemed by startled witnesses to have been pure magic. The story then progresses almost entirely by means of diverse conversations (*razmovy*) presented as short chapters that, for all the changes of scene, together form a satisfying whole. They mostly involve the eponymous young hero, including several with a wood dweller (*liasny dziadziuchna*) who advises him on life and, in particular, his amorous ambitions, in addition to several comic conversations with the nobles and local priests. By the end of the novella the enterprising kitchen boy Jalmužna has managed to get himself ennobled and wins the hand of his beloved. It is not, however, this romance or any other aspect of plot that gives the book its unique quality, but the text itself, which is rich in lexicon, imagery, epithets and swift changes of tone and mood, whilst remaining eminently readable throughout.

The purpose of the novella is not to retell historical facts so much as to recreate the spirit of the times by means of lively realistic and fantastic scenes, and very many exchanges between people of all ranks and stations; Bryĺ's character portrayal is masterly, as is the colourful yet authentic language of his personages. Most of the conversations include the quick-witted hero himself; his wide-ranging discussions, particularly with members of the clergy, introduce a rich vein of humour as well as an insight into the warp and woof of religious beliefs and superstitions at that time. The three quotations from this text that are reproduced here are, however, without him, but comprise only conversations between members of the aristocracy. The first, 'Razmova lia bramy' (Conversation near the gates), illustrates the ambient humour in the book; it is between two nobles, Lord Oĺbracht Haštaŭt and Prince Paval Haĺšanski. The latter wants to talk about the king of the hawks, but his companion seems sceptical and so begins to extol the merits of bees instead:

> 'Але я хацеў яшчэ расказаць табе пра пчалу. Пчала мае найсаладзейшы голас, і калі яна пяе, усе змаўкаюць і цешацца.'
>
> 'Ды ані каліва,' — перабіў Гаштаўт. — 'Пчала гудзе і мармыча, як п'яны францішканін, і хто не пачуе, так і сочыць, каб не джыганула выпадкам у руку ці ў шчаку.'
>
> 'Пэўна, што і праўда так,' — пагадзіўся князь Павал. — 'А яшчэ пчала заўжды мае патрэбу ў мёдзе, і паўсюль яго шукае, і рассылае ганцоў ва ўсе бакі, і распытвае сустрэчных, ці не бачылі яны дзе мёду, каб адтуль ужо прынесці ды скласці ў вуллі.'
>
> Гаштаўт нахмурыўся.
>
> 'Ты гэта жартуеш, родзіч, а ці звар'яцеў за кнігамі?' (Bryĺ 2014, 86)

> ('But I wanted to also tell you about a bee. A bee has a most sweet voice and when it sings everyone is silent and entertained.' 'Nothing of the kind', interrupted Haštaŭt. 'A bee drones and mutters like a drunken Franciscan friar, and as soon as anyone hears it, they watch out that it doesn't by chance sting them in the arm or cheek.' 'You're probably right' agreed Prince Paval. 'But a bee is always in need of honey, and looks for it everywhere, and sends couriers in all directions, and asks those he meets whether they have seen honey anywhere, in order to bring it from there and put it in the hive'. Haštaŭt frowned. 'You are joking now, relative, or have you gone crazy over your books?)

Another early conversation, 'Razmova miž fresak' (A conversation amongst the frescoes), is also worth illustrating. In one of Haštaŭt's rooms in the palace there are frescoes depicting the foundation of Litva (Bryĺ's word for the Grand Duchy of Lithuania). The owner proudly shows the pictures to Prince Paval, beginning with one of Nero and his relative Palaemon who is supposed to have originally come to Lithuania. These frescoes allow the author to extend his detailed historical portraits well beyond the Slav lands. Another fresco is set on the river Nioman where, it was believed, the country was founded (Bryĺ 2014, 33–36). As the nobles talk, Oĺbracht begins to lament the decline of his land in 1517:

> 'Але што рабіць, калі часы ідуць на спад, ідуць і да сёння? Год Панскі тысяча пяцьсот сямнаццаты — у самых гэтых словах чутная восень. І як лісты адрываюцца ўвосень ад дрэў, так і людскія цноты ўжо не могуць утрымацца разам, нават і ў рымлянах.' (Bryĺ 2014, 37)

> ('But what can be done?, when times are going into decline, even to the present day: The year of Our Lord 1517 — in these very words can be felt autumn. And just as leaves are torn from trees in autumn, in the same way people's honours can no longer hold together even amongst the Romans.')

This mention of the Romans leads to a general discussion of ancestry. Oĺbracht is sure that he descends from the Romans, but Paval counters that the French, English and Turks also claim ancient forebears. He is told, however, that these are all fairy tales:

> 'Але гэта казкі!' — абурыўся Гаштаўт. — 'Ці мала ў кнігах казак і ці мала казак у пагалосках?'
>
> 'А калі не з кніг ды пагалосак, то адкуль нам знаць і пра Літву?'. падхапіў князь.
>
> Гаштаўт бліснуў вачыма і падаўся наперад, быццам маючы на гэты выпад адказ з адказаў, але замёр, уздыхнуў, нахмурыўся і не сказаў зусім нічога. А князь Павал працягваў:
>
> 'Чаму б не быць Палемону казкай? Я чуў аб ім ад цябе — а ад каго чуў ты і чаму паверыў? Можа, проста камусьці здалося, што Рым далёка, а аб далёкім заўжды выдумляюць небывалае.' (Bryĺ 2014, 38)

> ('But those are fairy stories!', Haštaŭt was enraged. 'Are there few fairy stories in books and are there few fairy stories in rumours?' 'But if not from books or rumours, then how do we know about Lithuania?', rejoined the Prince. Haštaŭt's eyes flashed and he moved forward as if he had on this occasion an answer to end answers, but became rooted to the spot, sighed, frowned and said nothing. But Prince Paval continued: 'Why should not Palaemon also be a fairy story? I heard about him from you — but who did you hear it from and why did you believe it? Perhaps it just seemed to somebody that Rome was far away, and about faraway things people always think up fantastic stories')

Apart from the richly textured narratives and discussions, Bryĺ succeeds in making disparate 'conversations' into a whole picture of a fascinating period of Belarusian history through life in one medieval castle, with the combination of naivety and cunning, wit and stupidity and the use and abuse of power of the dwellers in and around it. *Jan Jalmužna* could never have been a historical novel, but as a novella it presents no less strong an impression of the past, combining fairy tale with rich humour, unfailingly vivid descriptions and excellent characterization.

Quite different, but also worthy of attention is *Historyja ŭ pryciemkach*[3] (History in the half-light) by Źmicier Dziadzienka (b. 1972), which contains three novellas, two of which are detective stories; the third, however, 'Jajki ptuški Ruch' (The eggs of the Roc bird) is an engaging and inventive historical fantasy. It opens with a Mongol torturing a bespectacled man (*akuliarnik* — 'Specky') in the vain hope of extracting from him the secret of where the Roc's eggs may be found. Imagining him to be a sculptor, he plans to damage his hands as punishment, but his victim turns out to be an art historian working on ancient documents, and the main part of the story is the scholar's rather wordy account to the Mongol of Belarusian history, coming back again and again to the subject of eggs, with which he had become obsessed (Dziadzienka, 5–11). He tells his tormentor (who writes everything down) of a Grand Duke at the time of the Grand Duchy of Lithuania who gave presents of eggs to the French King, to Pope Urban VIII and Peter the Great, as well as to some other aristocrats in the Grand Duchy. Amongst various legends, including that of Leda and the swan, and of the mysterious egg forming various monsters and gargoyles, is that the Ahinski family's eggs gave birth to beautiful statues, something that is echoed in the second part of the novella.

Here Specky tells how he had been followed to his flat by people looking for information about the legendary eggs (Dziadzienka, 11). Shortly afterwards a newspaper mysteriously appears in his letter box with an article about unauthorized statues in a park at the end of the 1920s which were rumoured to have come from some prehistoric bird. They are soon deemed to be anti-Soviet, and their sculptor is denounced as a spy and shot (Dziadzienka, 12–13). Specky thinks that the paper must have been sent by the KDB who appear to have already raided his flat, but he soon receives an anonymous phone call saying that 'they' know all about a search of his flat, offering him money for information about the eggs and his silence. Faced with this double threat and offer, Specky decides to burn all his papers, telling the Mongol what he has done and that he is very afraid of pain (Dziadzienka, 15). Then he lies on the floor in convulsions while the infuriated Mongol kicks and kicks him in frustration. Dziadzienka's book is a good example of fictionalized legend.

Sieviaryn Kviatkoŭski in 'Stračanaja staronka' (The lost page) is also about the search for missing information and material items. The narrator, who is, incidentally, obsessed by the significance of numbers, is dismayed by the lack of documents relating to Belarusian history, in particular the 'Polacak Chronicle' and wonders how it disappeared and why the Muscovites destroyed it (Kviatkoŭski, 79–80). An important part of this story is a disquisition on the relatively unknown history of religion in this region and particularly of the Khazars, including some historical mysteries, snippets from the history of the Khazars and their beliefs about hunters of dreams, not all of which come to pass (Kviatkoŭski, 83–85). The author relates various historical and mythical events from the conflict between Russians and Khazars, but ends on a somewhat bizarre note, stating that now they (he and others) can work on the Lithuanian Lexicon and thus live in their own Immortality (Kviatkoŭski, 87–88).

* * * * *

The period at the beginning of the twentieth century is represented in ludic form by the witty and imaginative Anka Upala, notably in two pieces about Belarus's national poets from her cycle 'Ukliasyki' (At the classics). The first is 'Jak Kolas i Kupala brali Smalenks' [*sic*] (How Kolas and Kupala captured Smalienks): the two poets go to Moscow on a diplomatic mission, hoping to get Smalenks back from the Russians to join Minks and Pinks, but during it they realize that the initials of the road from Pinks via Minks to Smalienks would be PMS (Premenstrual syndrome), so they abandon the idea of claiming Smalenks and go home. As in all of this writer's work there are many humorous details (Upala, 19–22). The other piece about the two poets emphasises their supposed rivalry: 'Kupaĺlie i Kalośsie' ([the feast of] Kupalle and Ears of corn), It opens with a phone call from Kupala to Kolas, in which the former absurdly informs the latter that the holiday of Kupaĺlie was in his (Kupala's) honour (Upala, 22). Amazed and disgruntled, Kolas also wants a holiday in his own honour. He goes to visit Karatkievič, who cannot think of a holiday for him, but changes the title of his novel *Kalasy pad siarpom tvaim* (Ears of Corn under Your Sickle, 1968) in the hope of satisfying his visitor (Upala, 22–27).[4] Again there is a series of absurdly comic details. Elements like the deliberate misspelling of Belarusian place names in the first piece, and the deliberate anachronism of the second are all part of this writer's stock in trade of imaginative, witty and highly readable writing, not all of which can find a place in the thematic chapters of the present work.

* * * * *

World War II

Several writers treat themes related to the topic of World War II, although they were all born well after its end. In verse Vitaĺ Ryžkoŭ (b. 1986), Adam Šostak (b. 1982), Siarhiej Prylucki (b. 1980) and Taćciana Niadbaj (b. 1982) were amongst those who wrote about the war.[5] Pages 6–57 of the pages of *Maladość*, 4 (2005) were devoted to the 60th anniversary of the end of World

War II, of which at least thirteen pages comprised stories and poems by Miensk schoolchildren, giving their impressions of this distant event. Three examples of the eight prose items will have to suffice: Julija Hiĺ's 'Čaravički' (Slippers) about her grandmother's introduction to the war; Voĺha Mieĺničenka's 'Pomsta' (Vengeance) on blowing up a railway line; and Kaciaryna Karpiej's 'Sustreča' (A meeting), which expresses gratitude to the Soviet soldiers.

Siarhiej Balachonaŭ is undoubtedly one of the leading young historical writers, and one of his stories, 'Paliavańnie na pačvarnaha parciuka' was considered in the first chapter, but his other stories, already discussed briefly in my *Writing in a Cold Climate*, are concerned with World War II, and will be discussed in a little more detail here. His best-known story is 'Śmierć liutenisty' (Death of a lutenist), which is presented as the tale of an old American (presumably an immigrant of some kind). Set in German-occupied Miensk, it depicts idealistic young Belarusians engaged in liberation politics, although the eponymous musician Anatoĺ Lahucionak, is kept to the periphery of their activities. During a failed assassination attempt he is killed and other deaths follow, although his demise is foreshadowed by earlier amorous rivalry, whether or not it was the actual cause of death:

> Вечарынка скончылася спакойна. Анатоль зусім не чапляўся да Ганны, хаця сам сабою зрабіўся відавочнаю зоркаю сьвята, дарма што бязь лютні. Міхась адно хітаў галавою: 'Ну-ну, спадару Лагуцёнак, як жа нам з вамі можна вадзіцца? Вы ж над меру вульканічны, дый жа там, дзе ня трэба'. (Balachonaŭ, 215)
>
> (The party ended peacefully. Anatoĺ did not attach himself to Hanna at all, although he had clearly become the star of the celebration, despite being without his lute. Michaś only nodded his head 'Well, well, Mr Lahucionak, what are we to do with you? You are excessively volcanic, and precisely where it is not needed'.)

Far more shocking is 'Piatnaccać lišnich chvilin' (Fifteen superfluous minutes), also set in occupied Belarus, in which a schoolteacher, Barys Aliaksiučyc, and his pupils give a Nazi salute and shout, 'Heil Hitler!', an act, though hateful and bizarre, is not altogether alien to his way of thinking, as may be seen from his earlier reflections:

> І сягоньня, калі магутнае нямецкае войска пад павадырствам вялікага Адольфа Гітлера аслабаніла Беларусь ад бальшавіцка-жыдоўскага паняволеньня, перад намі расчыніліся новыя далягляды ў працы і барацьбе. (Balachonaŭ, 177)
>
> (And today, when the powerful German forces under the leadership of the great Adolf Hitler has freed Belarus from Bolshevik-Jewish servitude, before us have opened new horizons of work and struggle.)

As might be expected, the story ends in betrayals and brutal deaths, and Balachonaŭ seemingly draws a moral equivalence between Stalin and Hitler, not uncommon in Belarusian and Russian émigré writing and occasionally mooted by bold Russian writers,[6] but rare indeed in Belarus itself.

Another difficult moral choice and sacrifice is featured in 'Second Security' in which a nationally conscious Belarusian, Aliaksandar Šaliuta, gives up his love and material wellbeing for the sake of a higher ideal. His thinking on national questions is both familiar and piquant:

> Ён ніяк ня мог уразумець, чаму на зямлі беларускай няма беларускіх гарадоў, чаму беларусы апынуліся пераважна за гарадзкою рысай — у вёсках, нібы амерыканскія індзейцы ў reservation. Гэта яго вельмі дапякала, бо меў геніяльную неасьцярожнасьць памысьліць пра стварэньне беларускай дзяржавы. (Balachonaŭ, 154–55)
>
> (He could not understand at all why in the Belarusian land there were no Belarusian cities, why Belarusians had mostly stayed outside the city boundaries — in villages, like American Indians in their reservations. This really plagued him, for he had the brilliant temerity to think about the creation of a Belarusian state.)

Balachonaŭ's bold reassessment of the traditional or official view of the War and the German occupation of Belarus is expressed in an extreme and fantastic way in 'Nie ruš majho strachu' (Do not move my fear) in which the German forces, the Russians led by the NKVD, as well as those fighting for an independent Belarus are all taken aback by the arrival of a visitor from another planet. He seems, moreover, to be familiar with the Belarusian language and local customs, and intervenes to make the possibility of an independent Belarus, if not a reality, at least more likely. Although this introduction of a fantastic element is not to all tastes, nonetheless Balachonaŭ stands out as an independently minded and highly original writer about Belarus's relatively recent past as well as ancient history.

Germany continues to fascinate some Belarusian writers. Taćciana Barysik (b. 1977), for instance, in her 'Usiu žyźniu uźnica' ('A prisoner for all her life') treats episodically a number of themes relating to the War and its aftermath, beginning with a fat psychologically sick war veteran, nicknamed Kamputer (Computer), who stands at the entrance of a tall building shouting 'Вайна!, Вайна! [...] 62 гады таму пачалася вайна!' (Barysik, 69) (War!, War! [...] War began 62 years ago!). In another short episode a group of Mahilioŭ children are in 1992 sent to Germany for their health, and a little boy causes consternation by singing an anti-Fascist song he had learned at school (Barysik, 69–70). There are various other tales of contacts with Germany, ranging from marriages with Germans to compensation for war crimes, including the contrast between propaganda and reality, and the question of help for war veterans from the

Belarusian authorities. The latter produces a comic exchange between local officials and a down-to-earth veteran:

> 'Якую вам трэба аказаць дапамогу?'
> 'Нічога мне ня трэба. Толькі вазок гною, агарод засеяць'
> 'Гэтага мы ня можам.'
> 'Ну, калі ўжо гаўно даць ня можаце, то й няма пра што гаварыць.' (Barysik, 72)
>
> ('What help do you need us to provide?'
> 'I don't need anything. Only a load of manure to put on my vegetable patch.'
> 'That we can't do.'
> 'Well, if you cannot even give me shit, then we have nothing to talk about.')

Sieviaryn Kviatkoŭski presents a decidedly unconventional aspect of partisan warfare. In his already mentioned 'Majskaja saha' (May saga) a Polish teacher (Panas) tells his (Belarusian) class about his wartime experiences, particularly the sexual ones. In a partisan division in 1943 (Kviatkoŭski, 34) Panas's favourite is an attractive woman, Kacia, who offers her services to many soldiers in their dugouts. Despite trouble with political officers from Moscow, she has become legendary by the time the Red Army arrives. Reputed to be syphilitic, she forms an attachment to Panas, and later becomes a teacher in his school (Kviatkoŭski, 43). The most improbable aspect of this virtuosic short story is undoubtedly the young audience to which these salacious reminiscences are addressed.

Finally may be mentioned Paval Kaściukievič's story 'Moj frantavy tavaryš Kurt Voniehut' (My comrade from the front, Kurt Vonnegut) in which he relates his childhood dreams of daring attacks on trains and so on, but later, visiting the Belarus film studios, he is disgusted to find that they are not only making films about the War, but also about all sorts of other *luchta* (rubbish). Playing back his childhood dreams, he is dismayed that he, his girl and other friends all seem to be dressed in the uniform of the SS, which, in fact, appears to resemble the Soviet officers' ones (Kaściukievič, 64–65). It was the (American and Belarusian) film makers after the War that made the Germans look so much more fashionable and elegant than their allies, so that half the soldiers in these films appeared to be SS (Kaściukievič, 65–66). The narrator does not feel guilty about his dreams, having been born long after the War, but wonders, with characteristic irony, who today's children are dreaming of killing (Kaściukievič, 66).

The varied depictions of World War II discussed above should be seen in the context not only of the immense number of Belarus's victims of the War, but also of the latter's importance as a central element in the present regime's ideology including the continued reference to it as the Great War of the Fatherland, apparently ignoring the period before the Soviet Union was invaded when the Molotov-Ribbentrop pact was in force (1939–1941), or indeed the continuing war with Japan in the East after the Germans had been defeated. Moreover, some half a century later in Belarus children are still being encouraged to write their impressions of this distant conflict.

* * * * *

Chernobyl

After all the understandably impassioned writing about the Chernobyl tragedy in Belarusian poetry like Ryhor Baradulin's 'Malitva nastupnaści' (Prayer of Accession, 1988) and Uladzimir Niakliajeŭ's 'Zona' (The Zone, 1986), to name but two of the most powerful works, as well as the extensive documentary works of, for example, Vasiĺ Jakavienka, it is, perhaps, surprising that in the sample of young prose here the only story about this landmark event in recent Belarusian history is Liolik Uškin's miniature, 'Sapraŭdnaja historyja Čarnobyliu' (The true history of Chernobyl), in which the tragedy (or, at least, the official reaction to it) is treated as a farce. A letter to a news editor about how well the victims of Chernobyl are living, thanks to the efforts of the authorities, is followed by some entertaining materials from supposed official reactions to these grim events:

> ЦК КПБ 27-ага красавіка 1986г.
>
> Першы сакратар: 'Шаноўныя таварышы, у мяне для вас дзьве навіны: добрая і дрэнная. У Чарнобылі накрыўся рэактар, на нас ідзе радыяцыйнае воблака. Вы самі разумееце, што значыць радыяцыя для развіцця рэгіёну: сталая падтрымка дзяржавы, інвестары, здаровы аптымізм...'
>
> Усе: 'Ну?'
>
> Першы сакратар 'З улікам укладу футбалістаў мінскага 'Дынама' і гандбалістаў сталічнага СКА ў развіццё савецкага спорту дарагі генсек Міхаіл Сяргеевіч дазволіў нам пасадзіць радыяцыйнае воблака над нашай рэспублікай.'
>
> Усе (*разам*): 'Ну супер! Вось яна, праява ленінскай нацыянальнай палітыцы [*sic*]! Слава роднай Партыі!'
>
> Першы сакратар: 'Цяпер дрэнная навіна: воблака дазволілі пасадзіць толькі адно. Масква хоча, каб нешта перапала Браншчыне: там таксама сяло трэба ўздымаць.'
>
> Усе: 'Мля...маскалі, ды яны яшчэ нам Смаленск не павярнулі, а ўжо давай ім наша воблака...' (Uškin, 42–43)

> (CC CPB [The Central Committee of the Communist Party of Belarus] 27 April 1986
>
> First Secretary: 'Honoured comrades, I have two pieces of news for you, one good and one bad. In Chernobyl the reactor has been closed,

a radioactive cloud is coming our way. You yourselves understand what radiation means for the development of the region: constant support from the state, investors, healthy optimism...' All: 'Well?' First Secretary: 'Bearing in mind the contribution of the Minsk football team 'Dynama' and the handball players of the capital's Army Sports Club to the development of Soviet sport, dear General Secretary Mikhail Sergeevich [Gorbachev] has permitted us to land the radioactive cloud above our republic' All: 'Well, super! That's it, a manifestation of Lenin's nationality policy! Glory to our dear Party!' First Secretary: 'Now for the bad news: they have allowed only one cloud to fall on us. Moscow wants something to fall on the Briansk region: there too there is a need to raise the level of the villages.' All: 'Rud... Russkis, they still haven't returned Smaliensk to us, and now they also want to give them our cloud...')

* * * * *

History has been said to be too serious to leave to historians, but the examples of young prose illustrated in this chapter present, alongside the traditional albeit provocative works of Balachonaŭ, some other imaginative and irreverent, often humorous, depictions of various corners of ancient history and the relatively recent past. In a land where memory and history have had to be fought for to save them from being crushed under the forces of ignorance and indifference, the part played by even the most comic responses to historic events, old and new, supports the invaluable work of writers like Uladzimir Karatkievič and Uladzimier Arloŭ as well as professional historians such as Hienadź Sahanovič. Although history has not been deliberately denigrated and hindered in the way that the Belarusian language has, nonetheless it was grossly distorted during the Soviet period, and there is a lack of full documentation due to the disappearance of historical records. Thus its treatment in fiction as well as in scholarly works is important for keeping national identity fully alive in our prosaic and materialistic times.

Notes to Chapter 6

1. Anton Frańcišak Bryĺ, *Nie ŭpaŭ žolud* (Minsk: Lohvinaŭ 2011), pp. 42–43.
2. Anton Frańcišak Bryĺ, *Jan Jalmužna* (Minsk: Knihazbor, 2014) (hereafter Bryĺ 2014).
3. Źmicier Dziadzienka, *Historyja ŭ pryciemkach* (Minsk: Knihazbor, 2015) (hereafter Dziadzienka).
4. The idea of Karatkievič changing the title of his novel has another level, of which Upala was doubtless fully aware. The novel was, of course, originally published in two parts in 1965 (although planned to be in four), and the present title for the whole work was first used in 1968.
5. For more information on these poets see *SS*.
6. A prominent example was Vasilii Grossman (1905–1964), *Zhizn' i sud'ba* (Life and fate), published in full only in 1990.

SUMMARY

Naturally, there can be no easy summary of a work describing young writers at the beginning of their careers, many with much to offer in future. Nonetheless, one clear conclusion is that Belarusian literature, despite the unpromising climate in which it exists, continues to flourish. It was tempting to end this survey with the optimistic *All's Well that Ends Well* or, to continue the Shakespearean leitmotiv (what would that zealous genius Richard Wagner have said?), with Hector's depressing lines from *Troilus and Cressida*, 'that old common arbitrator, Time, / Will one day end it'.[1] That, however, would be to put the cart before the horse, in other words, to emphasise the chronicler rather than the youthful writers and their words that have been treated here. Some of the youngest come from an excellent anthology edited by poet Viktar Šnip, *Moj dzień pačynajecca* (My day is beginning), and a few from a collection of writing about World War II by schoolchildren invited (or perhaps dragooned) into writing essays and stories about an event that ended over seventy years earlier, but which continues to form a central part of the present regime's ideological baggage. Several of the other stories come from various collections of prize-winners' works, or those collected on political (if that is the right word for feminist) principles. Most of the texts, however, are published in a range of individual books.

This short volume is the final part of the present writer's attempts to make Belarus known in the outside world, not only for Chernobyl and for being what Condoleeza Rice called 'the last dictatorship in Europe', but also for its rich cultural history, particularly literature, that began with the first Slav biblical translations and commentaries by Francis Skaryna (c.1490 — c.1551), and is now continuing strongly, in many cases not only as a response to creative impulses, but also as a counter to general ignorance of the Belarusian cultural heritage and, concomitant to it, low national consciousness. Having come to this literary wealth by chance nearly half a century ago,[2] I have been greatly encouraged by the kindness, modesty and generosity of the people of the country, and privileged to know some of the greatest Belarusian writers and poets as well as many of the younger ones, as well as critics and translators in this economically poor but spiritually rich central European country.

To repeat the immortal words of national poet Janka Kupala (1882–1947):

'Long Live Belarus!'

1. Shakespeare, *Troilus and Cressida*, IV, v,224–25.
2. As a research student under the inspired tutelage of Professor Robert Auty.

BIBLIOGRAPHY

Adamovič, Andrej, *Taŭścila i liešč* (Minsk: Lohvinaŭ, 2015) (in text Adamovič)
Aksak, Valiańcina, ed., *Vierš na svabodu* (Prague: Radyjo Svaboda, 2002)
Aliaškievič, Marharyta, 'Taŭstuha', *Plp*, pp. 23–30 (in text Aliaškievič)
Astapova, Anastasiya, *Negotiating Belarusianness: Political Folklore Betwixt and Between* (Tartu: University of Tartu Press, 2015)
Astrašeŭski, Kastuś, and Ludwik Burakoŭski, comps, *Idyjot samy nastajaščy* (Minsk-Warsaw-Moscow: Kontra-Press, 2000). Second, enlarged edition, 2001
Babina, Natalka, and others, comps, *Žančyny vychodziać z-pad kantroliu: Bielaruskaje žanočaje apaviadańnie* (Minsk: Lohvinaŭ, 2007) (in text *Žvzpk*)
Bajarovič, Žmicier, *Šali: Liryčna-pobytavaja proza* (Minsk: Halijafy, 2012) (in text Bajarovič)
Balachonaŭ, Siarhiej, *Imia hrušy: Raman, apaviadańni* (Minsk: Lohvinaŭ, 2005) (in text Balachonaŭ)
Banduryna, Kryścina, 'Śliady na čystaj papiery', *Mdp*, pp. 29–32 (in text Banduryna)
Baradulin, Ryhor, 'Malitva nastupnaści', *Treba być doma ćaściej* (Minsk: Mastackaja litaratura, 1993), pp. 278–79
Barysik, Taćciana, 'Kachańnie ŭ našym kuście', *Žvzpk*, pp. 58–64 (in text Barysik)
Barysiuk, Taćciana, 'Formula žanočaha ščaścia ŭ šliubie (*antyparady*)', *Litaraturny ekvatar: Aĺmanach*, 5 (2016), 25
Bennett, Brian, *The Last Dictatorship in Europe: Belarus Under Lukashenko* (London: Hurst and Co, 2011)
Bielanožka, Aliona, 'Maladzik pa niebie chodzić' *Mdp*, pp. 42–48 (in text Bielanožka)
Biziajeva, Alisa, 'Zdani prytomnaści', *Dziejasloŭ*, 2 (81) (2016), 180–83
Bryĺ, Anton Frańcišak, *Nie ŭpaŭ žolud* (Minsk: Lohvinaŭ, 2011)
——*Jan Jalmužna* (Minsk: Knihazbor, 2014)
Bulgakov, Mikhail, *Master i Margarita*, first uncut edition (Frankfurt: Posev, 1969)
Byčkoŭski, Alieś, *Horad za 101-m kilamietram* (Minsk: Lohvinaŭ, 2004) (in text Byčkoŭski)
Chadanovič, Andrej, comp., *Hienijuš loci: Konkurs maladych litaratataraŭ da stahoddzia Larysy Hienijuš* (Minsk: Lohvinaŭ, 2012) (in text *Hienijuš loci*)
——*Ptuški liohkich pavodzinaŭ: Vieršy, proza i pieraklady finalistaŭ konkursu maladych litaratataraŭ imia Česlava Milaša* (Minsk: Lohvinaŭ, 2013) (in text *Plp*)
Charužka, Aliaksiej, 'Adzinota', *Pamiž*, 4 (2004–05), 54–58

CHARYTANIUK, NATALKA, 'Furmanka śviatoha Mikoly: Siamiejnyja ŭspaminy pra sustreču sa śviatym Mikolam na darozie miž Bieraściem i Vysokim uzimku 1941 hodu', *Žvzpk*, pp. 237–47 (in text Charytaniuk)

CROCE, BENEDETTO, *The Essence of Aesthetics* (London: William Heinemann, 1921)

ČUBAT, ALIAKSIEJ, *Hliniany čalaviek* (Minsk: Halijafy, 2008)

DANILIEVIČ, ANDRUŚ, 'Mara pra pryhožaje kachańnie', *Mdp*, pp. 74–76

—— 'Źnička', *Mdp*, pp. 76–77

DUBOŬSKI, KIRYLA, 'Bielaruskaja mova', *Hienijuš loci*, p. 85

—— 'Trubačka', *Hienijuš loci*, p. 86

DZIADZIENKA, ŹMICIER, *Historyja ŭ pryciemkach* (Minsk: Knihazbor, 2015) (in text Dziadzienka)

DŽECI, 'Jaźminičny Kaliadki', *Žvzpk*, pp. 114–24 (in text Džeci)

FILON, NADZIEJA, *Kropli śviatla* (Minsk: TAA 'Charviest', 2012)

GOGOL, NIKOLAI VASILEVICH, 'Nos', *Sovremennik*, 3 (1836), 54–90

HAPIEJEVA, VOĹHA, *Rekanstrukcyja nieba* (Minsk: Lohvinaŭ, 2003)

HARBACKI, ULADŹ, *Pieśni traliebusnych rahuliaŭ: Kazki i proza žyćcia* (London: belarusians.co.uk, 2016) (in text Harbacki)

HARBACKI, ULADZISLAŬ, *Ab feminizacyi bielaruskaj movy: Feminizacyja nomina agentis i peŭnych inšych katehoryjaŭ u sučasnaj bielaruskaj movie. Ese* (Leicester: belarusians.co.uk, 2012)

—— *Hid pa feminizacyi bielaruskaj movy (Nomina agentis i niekatorych inšych asabovych naminacyjaŭ* (Viĺnia: belarusians.co.uk, 2016)

HARRIS, JOANNE, *Five Quarters of the Orange* (New York: Doubleday, 2001)

HEMINGWAY, ERNEST, *The Old Man and the Sea* (New York: Scribner, 1952)

HUD, ŹMICIER, *Poŭdzień-3* (Minsk: Halijafy, 2013)

INGE, W.R. *Outspoken Essays*, Second series (London: Longmans Green and Co., 1922)

IVAŠČANKA, ANATOĹ, *Vieršnick* (Minsk: Biellitfond, 2006)

—— *Anatalohija*, Minsk: Knihazbor, 2015 (in text Ivaščanka)

JAKUĆ, PAVAL, 'Dziakuj', *Mdp*, pp. 49–50

JEMIALIANAŬ-ŠYLOVIČ, ALIEŚ, *Parasoniečnaść* (Minsk: Knihazbor, 2013)

—— 'Teliepaetyka: Rytaryčnyja adkazy', *Dziejasloŭ*, 4 (71) (2014), 62 (in text Jemialianaŭ)

KACIURHINA, ANASTASIJA, 'Čužoje žyćcio', *Mdp*, pp. 128–29

KAČATKOVA, PAŬLINA, 'Čužoje hniazdo', *Žvzpk*, pp. 139–43 (in text Kačatkova)

KALIENDA, SIARHIEJ, *Pomnik atručanym liudziam* (Minsk: Halijafy, 2009) (in text Kalienda)

KARATKIEVIČ, ULADZIMIR, *Chrystos pryziamliŭsia u Harodni: Jevanhieĺlie ad Judy* (Minsk: Mastackaja litaratura, 1966)

—— *Kalasy pad siarpom tvaim* (Minsk: Mastackaja litaratura, 1968)

KAŚCIUKIEVIČ, PAVAL, *Zbornaja RB pa niehaloŭnych vidach sportu* (Minsk: Lohvinaŭ, 2011) (in text Kaściukievič)

KAVALIEŬSKI, ARCIOM, *Admyslovyja huĺni* (Minsk: Lohvinaŭ, 2003)

—— *Addalienaść i addanaść: Paezija i liryčnaja proza* (Minsk: Halijafy, 2008) (in text Kavalieŭski)

KURČANKOVA, KRYŚCINA, 'Što-koĺviečy pra haradskich eĺfaŭ', *Žvzpk*, pp. 144–52 (in text Kurčankova)

KVIATKOŬSKI, SIEVIARYN, *Padarunak dlia Adeli* (Minsk: Lohvinaŭ, 2012) (in text Kviatkoŭski)

LATYŠKIEVIČ, MARHARYTA, 'Tumannaść miortvaj halavy', *Mdp*, pp. 148–55 (in text Latyškievič)

MCMILLIN, ARNOLD, 'Small is Sometimes Beautiful: Studying 'Minor' Languages at University with Particular Reference to Belarus: The Presidential Address of the Modern Humanities Research Association', *Modern Language Review*, 101.4 (2006), xxxii -xliii

—— *Writing in a Cold Climate: Belarusian Literature from the 1970s to the Present Day*, Publications of the Modern Humanities Research Association, 18 (London: Maney Publishing for the MHRA, 2010)

—— *Piśmienstva ŭ chalodnym klimacie: Bielaruskaja litaratura ad 70-ch hh. XX st. da našych dzion* (Białystok: Orthdruk, 2011)

—— *Spring Shoots: Young Belarusian Poets in the Early Twenty-First Century*, Publications of the Modern Humanities Research Association, 19 (Cambridge: MHRA, 2015) (in text *SS*)

—— *Ruń: Maladyja bielaruskija paety pačatku XXI stahoddzia* (Minsk: Knihazbor, 2016) (in text *Ruń*)

—— 'Macaronic Writing by Young Belarusian Poets: The Attraction of English "Barbarisms"', *Przegląd wschodnioeuropejski*, VII/2 (2016), 197–207 (in text McMillin Macaronic)

—— 'Pradstaŭnik redkaj dynastyi: Anton Fraṅcišak Bryĺ', *Polymia*, 11 (2016) (in text McMillin Bryĺ)

MALIAŬKA, MARYJA, 'Žyvaja ryba', *Dziejasloŭ*, 2 (81) (2006), 188–92 (in text Maliaŭka)

MANCEVIČ, NASTA, *Ptuški* (Minsk: Lohvinaŭ, 2012) (in text Mancevič)

MARTA, 'List pra kachańnie', *Žvzpk*, pp. 153–57 (in text Marta)

MARTYNOVIČ, JAŬHIEN, 'jon i jana', *Mdp*, pp. 197–98

—— 'Siem rečaŭ, jakija ja nie budu rabić, kali vyrastu. List u budučyniu', *Mdp*, pp. 199–201

—— 'Mora', *Mdp*, pp. 201–03.

MARTYSIEVIČ, MARYJA, *Cmoki liatuć na nierast* (Minsk: Lohvinaŭ, 2008)

MITCHELL, MARGARET, *Gone with the Wind* (New York, Macmillan, 1936)

MORT, VAĹŽYNA, *Ja tonieńkaja, jak tvaje viejki* (Minsk: Lohvinaŭ, 2005)

NIAKLIAJEŬ, ULADZIMIR, 'Zona', *Prošča* (Minsk: Krynica, Mastackaja litaratura, 1996), pp. 127–40

PALAČANSKI, ALIAKSIEJ, *Moj ćvik* (Minsk: Halijafy, 2014) (in text Palačanski)

PALAZKOVA, LARYSA, 'Dva apaviadańni', *Maladość*, 1 (2005), 8–10

ROŬDA, MARYJA, *Kliničny vypadak, aĺbo Daremnyja ŭcioki* (Minsk: Knihazbor, 2015) (in text Roŭda)

SADOŬSKI, ULADZIMIR, 'Zvyčaj', *Mdp*, pp. 253–56 (in text Sadoŭski)

SAROTNIK, VALIERYJA, 'Vosiem kazak dlia daroslych', *Žvzpk*, pp. 260–68 (in text Sarotnik)

SHAKESPEARE, WILLIAM, *The Arden Shakespeare: Complete Works*, ed. by Richard Proudfoot, Ann Thompson and David Scott Kastan (London, New Delhi, New York, Sydney: Bloomsbury, 1998)

SKARYNKINA, TANIA, *Šmat Česlava Milaša, krychu Elvisa Presli: Ese napisanyja dlia 'Budźma' ŭ 2014–2015* (Minsk: Lohvinaŭ, 2015)

STASIEĹKA, KIRYL, *Dziciačy manifiest* (Minsk: Halijafy, 2015) (in text Stasieĺka)

ŠNIP, VIKTAR (comp.), *Moj dzień pačynajecca: Proza i paezija maladych* (Minsk: Mastackaja litaratura, 2015) (in text *Mdp*)

ŠYBUT, HANNA, 'Śviatlo i ciemra', *Mdp*, pp. 328–31

—— 'Samy liepšy tata ŭ śviecie', *Mdp*, pp. 331–32

TOLSTOI, LEV NIKOLAEVICH, *Istoriia moego detstva* (St Petersburg: Sovremennik, 1852)

UMIEC, STANISLAVA, 'Abarani maje sny', *Mdp*, pp. 283–91 (in text Umiec)

UPALA, ANKA, *Dreva entalipt* (Minsk: Lohvinaŭ, 2012) (in text Upala)

UŠKIN, LIOLIK, *Jak adradzić VKL (fielietony, humareski)* (Minsk: Biblijatečka Centraĺnaja, 2016) (in text Uškin)

VOLKAŬ, MIKITA, 'Daroha damoŭ', *Mdp*, pp. 70–73 (in text Volkaŭ)

WILSON, ANDREW, *Belarus: The Last European Dictatorship* (New Haven and London: Yale University Press, 2011)

INDEX OF NAMES

www.ingramcontent.com/pod-product-compliance
Lightning Source LLC
Chambersburg PA
CBHW070546310726
48982CB00004B/853

* 9 7 8 1 7 8 1 8 8 7 7 0 7 *